Translating Borrowed Tongues

This book sheds light on the translations of renowned semiotician, essayist, and author Ilan Stavans, elucidating the ways in which they exemplify the migrant experience and translation as the interactions of living and writing in intercultural and interlinguistic spaces.

While much has been written on Stavans' work as a writer, there has been little to date on his work as a translator, subversive in their translations of Western classics such as *Don Quixote* and *Hamlet* into Spanglish. In Stavans' experiences as a writer and translator between languages and cultures, Vidal locates the ways in which writers and translators who have experienced migratory crises, marginalization, and exclusion adopt a hybrid, polydirectional, and multivocal approach to language seen as a threat to the status quo. The volume highlights how the case of Ilan Stavans uncovers unique insights into how migrant writers' nonstandard use of language creates worlds predicated on deterritorialization and in-between spaces which more accurately reflect the nuances of the lived experiences of migrants.

This book will be of particular interest to students and scholars in translation studies, literary translation, and Latinx literature.

MªCarmen África Vidal Claramonte is Full Professor of Translation at the University of Salamanca, Spain. Her research interests include translation theory, migration studies, post-structuralism, post-colonialism, contemporary art, and gender studies. She has published 17 books, 12 edited volumes, and over 100 articles and book chapters on these issues. She is a practising translator specialized in the fields of philosophy, literature, history, and contemporary art.

Routledge Focus on Translation and Interpreting Studies

Translation and Social Media Communication in the Age of the Pandemic
Edited by Tong King Lee and Dingkun Wang

Translating Borrowed Tongues
The Verbal Quest of Ilan Stavans
MᵃCarmen África Vidal Claramonte

For more information about this series, please visit: https://www.routledge.com/Routledge-Focus-on-Translation-and-Interpreting-Studies/book-series/RFTIS

Translating Borrowed Tongues

The Verbal Quest of Ilan Stavans

MªCarmen África Vidal Claramonte

Routledge
Taylor & Francis Group

NEW YORK AND LONDON

First published 2023
by Routledge
605 Third Avenue, New York, NY 10158

and by Routledge
4 Park Square, Milton Park, Abingdon, Oxon, OX14 4RN

Routledge is an imprint of the Taylor & Francis Group, an informa business

© 2023 MªCarmen África Vidal Claramonte

Library of Congress Cataloging-in-Publication Data
Names: Vidal, M. Carmen Africa, author.
Title: Translating borrowed tongues: the verbal quest of Ilan Stavans/Ma.
Carmen África Vidal Claramonte.
Description: New York, NY: Routledge, 2023. |
Series: Routledge focus on translation and interpreting studies | Includes bibliographical references and index.
Identifiers: LCCN 2022021960 (print) | LCCN 2022021961 (ebook) |
ISBN 9781032347622 (hardback) | ISBN 9781003323730 (ebook)
Subjects: LCSH: Stavans, Ilan. | Translating and interpreting.
Classification: LCC P306.92.S73 V53 2023 (print) | LCC P306.92.S73 (ebook) |
DDC 418/.02092–dc23/eng/20220627
LC record available at https://lccn.loc.gov/2022021960
LC ebook record available at https://lccn.loc.gov/2022021961

ISBN: 9781032347622 (hbk)
ISBN: 9781032347639 (pbk)
ISBN: 9781003323730 (ebk)

DOI: 10.4324/9781003323730

Typeset in Times New Roman
by Deanta Global Publishing Services, Chennai, India

Contents

Preface

In Book Four of the *Odyssey*, Menelaus is told that he might learn his fate if he succeeds in wrestling into submission the shapeshifting sea god Proteus. Menelaus' task proves almost impossible, as Proteus keeps slithering out of his grasp, assuming the forms of a lion, a serpent, a leopard, a pig, water, and a tree.

Ilan Stavans is as elusive a target as Proteus. Critic, essayist, professor, editor, publisher, translator, interviewer, lexicographer, memoirist, fiction-writer, poet, filmmaker – continuously migrating among those categories, Stavans refuses to accept a unitary identity. A migrant from Mexico to the United States, he is at home in not being at home; "Restless Books" is the name he gave the publishing house he founded. He refuses to limit himself to any one of the five languages he cherishes most – Spanish, Yiddish, Hebrew, English, and Spanglish. He has a kabbalistic infatuation with the power of words and knows them to be polysemous and indeterminate. Stavans recognizes and relishes the fact that language is a verb not a noun, an unstable, fluid energy. He is particularly drawn to demotic, hybrid tongues such as Yiddish and Spanglish that embody the vitality of changing cultures.

When I published *The Restless Ilan Stavans: Outsider on the Inside* in 2019, I recognized that no single volume could contain the multitudes that Stavans embodies. And no scholar but Stavans himself could match him in his range of skills and interests. I also recognized that, given his stunning productivity – more books in one year than most writers produce in a dec-ade – any attempt to summarize his work would have to be provisional as long as he continued to breathe. *Duma spirat scribit.* So in the scant three years since my book appeared, Stavans has produced books on Yiddish in America; the *Popol Vuh*; COVID-19; Jewish Latin America; Jewish litera-ture; *Alicia's Adventuras en Wonderlandia*, his translation into Spanglish of the Lewis Carroll classic; and a collection of Stavans' translations of poetry.

A prolific scholar of translation whose productivity almost matches her subject's, África Vidal Claramonte is the ideal writer to examine Stavans for Spanish-speaking readers. In her study of him, she has wisely chosen to focus on Stavans the translator, the translingual immigrant writer who has declared that he lives in translation and who, following his beloved Borges, insists that everything is a translation, that there are no originals. Translation is at the heart of most of Stavans' activities, not merely his explicit transposing of texts from one language to another. In that, he has been ambitious and even brazen, working into or out of not only Spanish, English, Yiddish, Hebrew, and Spanglish, languages he knows well. But he has also exhibited the chutzpah to take on texts from languages he does not know, such as Russian, German, Portuguese, even K'iche'. Beyond that, though, Stavans' work as interviewer, editor, essayist, and, especially, teacher fulfils his continuing mission of intermediation. Referring to his role of explaining Latino culture to non-Latinos, Jewish culture to non-Jews, he once referred to himself as *un puente*. África Vidal Claramonte is a lucid and insightful bridge to that bridge.

Steven G. Kellman

Acknowledgements

I would like to express my thanks to Steven G. Kellman for writing the prologue and for his support.

I would also like to thank the University of Salamanca for the funding given to the research group GIR TRADIC, *Translation, ideology, culture*, within whose framework all of my research on Ilan Stavans has been carried out.

I am especially grateful to Elysse Preposi, the admirably professional editor of the Routledge Focus series. Her attentiveness has resulted in a trouble-free publication process.

Introduction

Writing about Ilan Stavans and his work opens the door to an almost infinite universe, which is vividly portrayed in the rich spectrum of subjects and topics addressed. He has rewritten archetypal stories such as the *Popol Vuh*, an ancient oral text of the Mayas, and provided insights into figures as diverse as Octavio Paz, Raúl Zurita, Pablo Neruda, Don Quixote, Jorge Luis Borges, Julio Cortázar, Gabriel García Márquez, José Vasconcelos, Óscar "Zeta" Acosta, and Cantinflas. His book on Sor Juana Inés de la Cruz reveals her both as a literary figure and as a pop icon. He has published studies on Latin American and Jewish literature as well as on Latino art. His richly nuanced work explores the pre-Columbian bestiary of fantastic creatures in Latin America, Lazarillo de Tormes, and the significance of being Hispanic. Other topics that he has focused on include soap operas, food, selfies, memes, and even soccer and baseball. The list is endless.

Stavans' literary production comprises poetry, prose, and graphic novels. His writings reflect his immersion in popular culture and high culture, both of which are equally important in his eyes. One of the staunchest defenders of Spanglish, Stavans has been translated into 20 languages. Some of his work has even been adapted for cinema, television, theatre, and radio. Not surprisingly, he has been the topic of various books, such as *The Restless Ilan Stavans: Outsider on the Inside* (2019) by Steven Kellman, and *The Critic between Two Canons* (2019) edited by Bridget Kevane. Stavans has also been the subject of many academic papers that analyze his translations, essays, novels, and poems. These publications reflect the interesting debates that he and his literature have generated. Authors from all over the world discuss his controversial literary analyses and seek to explain why he has included certain works and authors in his anthologies but not others.

Nevertheless, despite the enormous variety of topics addressed in Stavans' work, in my opinion the two cornerstones that underlie all this diversity are language and then translation, or both, since they are the same thing. Precisely for this reason and because all of his literary work cannot

DOI: 10.4324/9781003323730-1

be satisfactorily addressed in one volume, this book focuses on Stavans' facet as a translator.

This is the Stavans who lives, both literally and metaphorically, on the border between languages. In fact, I see him as a translated translator, some-one that is perpetually engaged and immersed in the process of transla-tion. Like language and languages, he is restless, in constant movement and flux, travelling back and forth between different languages and cultures – Latino, Jewish, American, Hebrew, Yiddish, Mexican, Spanish, English, and Spanglish. Books such as *Immigration* (2008), *Words in Transit* (2016), and *The Wall* (2018), *inter alia*, reflect his deep social concern not only for contemporary migrations, a situation in which translation plays an impor-tant role, but also for languages, art, food, sports, and many other issues.

Translation is pervasive in our globalized society. In her introduction to a monographic issue of the *Philological Quarterly*, A. E. B. Coldiron (2016) gives an excellent description of what translation involves in today's world. From the very beginning, she argues that a translation is by defini-tion an interpretation, a rereading, and a rewriting. This signifies that every translation recreates the source text, and transforms it into something new, a process that is infinitely more complex than simply reformulating the text in another language.

This new perspective is the natural result of the cultural turn in Translation Studies, which began in the 1990s with Susan Bassnett and André Lefevere. It was partly triggered by Theo Hermans' 1985 edited volume on trans-lation as manipulation, and another by Lefevere's 1992 book on transla-tion as rewriting. Their work augured changes in translation, which would finally give translators a voice, and their work, the status that it deserved. No longer regarded as the curse of Babel or enslaved by absolute equiva-lence, translation was transformed. It emerged from its cocoon with butter-fly wings and became a fascinating quest into the multidimensional world of language and creativity.

An extremely revealing detail in Anne Coldiron's text (2016: 315) is that she refers to the texts to be translated not as the "originals" but rather as their "prior texts". Her rejection of the binary opposition of original text and translation is indicative of how she conceives translation, which coincides with the view of many other contemporary authors. This position on transla-tion has important implications.

At the end of the first section of *El Aleph*, Borges writes that the "pobre limosna que en ocasiones nos dejan las horas y los días son las palabras de los otros, desplazadas y mutilada".[1] As translators, we have no choice but to use those displaced and mutilated words, not to produce a secondary text but rather to write a new one that is created after the prior text. Those words are the keys that allow us to study and decode the original text, and ultimately open the door to the new world revealed through its translation. Those words allow us to understand the extent to which the manipulated and abraded world of the previous text can ultimately be used to provide a meaningful foundation for the new one.

When we acknowledge the independence of the translated text, the original is no longer the first or source text. Instead, it is relegated to the status of a prior text. Our view thus coincides with that of Borges, who observes that translation completes the original. This signifies that in regard to fidelity, it is the original that is unfaithful to the translation, and not vice versa. Translating is thus infinitely more complex than simply pouring meaning from one language into another. Instead, it is a fascinating activity that is directly linked to identity, space, and movement. In essence, it is not settling for being Pierre Menard.

Consequently, this unique view of the translation process lies at the centre of this book. The multiplicity of languages spoken throughout the world, far from being a curse, is an endless source of enrichment. In fact, as observed in the first chapter, Stavans is one of the clearest examples of a translingual writer (Kellman 2019) in the post-monolingual era, which is the literary context of his work.

This translingual literature pushes language to its limits because it is a reflection of contemporary hybridization. In one of his most recent books, it is no coincidence that Stavans (2021b: viii–ix), describes literature as the best window to scrutinize human contradictions. In the same book he stresses that "American literature is, first and foremost, the words it is made of. Those words are in eternal flux. They are nervous; they are disobedient; they never stay still" (*ibid.*: 89). As stated in the first chapter, the same is true of translingual literature in general.

Subsequent chapters focus on Stavans' identity(ies), his use of language(s), and how translation and self-translation are a constant in his life and work. The objective is to scrutinize the reverse side of the tapestry where the figures can barely be perceived because of the threads or to travel to the other side the looking glass. "La translación nunca es un innocent act: traducir es to interpret; es, also, subvertir" (Stavans 2021d: v).

This book portrays Stavans not only as a double agent (Stavans 2012), but also as a high-wire artist like Philippe Petit. In the same way as Petit, Stavans also performs a delicate balancing act, as he carefully walks between languages to magically accomplish a seemingly impossible feat on a linguistic tightrope. And in the same way as Petit's friends, who helped him to secretly rig his wire so that he could traverse the sky, he has no choice but to duplicate his identities in order to surreptitiously enter other spaces, which he would otherwise not be permitted to enter.

With the *morisco alijamiado* (Spanish-speaking Moor) in the manuscript that Cervantes happened upon by chance, Stavans can be found in *The Garden of Forking Paths*. He is also present in "The Thousand and One Nights", the story in *Seven Nights*, in which Borges asserts that

> stories within stories create a strange effect, almost infinite, a sort of vertigo. This has been imitated by writers ever since the "Alice" books of Lewis Carroll or his novel *Sylvia and Bruno*, where there are dreams that branch out and multiply.
>
> (Borges 1980/1984: 573)

These stories within stories, the countless books in *One and a Thousand Nights*, *Don Quixote*, *Sylvia and Bruno*, and so many other literary works, fascinate Borges, but also Stavans, who does not hesitate to confess his admiration for the Argentinian author.

What underlies Stavans' work is his vision of language as something that is more than a simple instrument of communication. Language instead constitutes an intricate labyrinth of signs that form a network of crossroads, which are different yet the same. Each language is a separate universe that has its own unique flavours, colours, and music. In Stavans' universe, languages (in the plural) create a de-hierarchized space where they continuously interact with each other. Thanks to translation, this space is used to construct new spaces and facilitate encounters since each word is a kind of Pandora's Box streaming reflections of remnants of the past and visions of the future.

Translating Borrowed Tongues: The Verbal Quest of Ilan Stavans is also a palimpsest, because it arose from *Ilan Stavans, traductor* (2022), a book originally published in Spain. To use Stavans' terminology, it is a non-equivalent translation, a second original. It expands the previous volume by analyzing translations of works such as the *Popol Vuh*. This book is about people who live in borrowed tongues (Karpinski 2012) and about an author living within his borrowed words (Stavans 2002). These words are an integral part of his life and his way of existing in the world. *Translating Borrowed Tongues: The Verbal Quest of Ilan Stavans* conceives words and languages as a challenge to the cultural and vital imperialism of the "major" languages (Karpinski 2012: 2). The assumption is that we learn from each new translation, and that translation "has its place in the production of new hybridities, new linkages between the local, the nation, and the global [...] migrancy and translation are inextricably linked" (Karpinski 2012: 1). Borrowed words show us that "language and culture are not stable entities with fixed boundaries but rather categories that are already plural and divided within, leaking and contaminated, open to flux and fusion" (Karpinski 2012: 3).

Writing a book means listening to many melodies and discovering hundreds of rhythms different from one's own. As we all know, researching any author or any idea means venturing into a huge library, where each volume surprises and enchants us, opening our minds to new ideas. In the case of Ilan Stavans, this is doubly true. Writing is a fascinating process because, as Borges so aptly observes, reading is a form of happiness. That is why writing about an author, such as Stavans, whose library contains practically all the translations of *Don Quixote*, has been an incredible adventure that has opened my eyes to multiple spaces and my ears to voices that have suggested alternative paths or crossroads of which I was previously unaware.

Publishing this book in English signifies understanding that the meaning of each word expresses different emotions in the new language. It involves reflecting on the fact that language is closely linked to identity, or rather to identities and emotions that are not always evident, like the figures barely perceived on the thread-ridden reverse side of a Flemish tapestry.

From Stavans I have also learnt that language is stereophonic, and that it is a way of life and of living in the world. He has shown me that words are never linear, but rather are composed of a myriad of interwoven threads from which no single meaning ever emerges. And so this version of the previous book is different because each time that Stavans is reread, new paths and new quests emerge.

Writing about a palimpsestic author is a never-ending task. Stavans continues to evolve and transform himself. His previous creations invariably point to uncharted territory that must be explored. To write this new book, I had to carefully listen to my previous one. And so I travelled to the other side of the looking glass on a quest to find all the stories in the hope that they would come to me. In the case of Ilan Stavans (and Alice), the number of stories is infinite, ninety times nine. I am aware, therefore, that this book is also incomplete. Indeed, if this quest has taught me anything, it is that it is impossible to confine Stavans, enclosing him in only a few pages. Dwelling in the house of mirrors means accepting the inversion of stories and resolving to never stop living adventures in language.

Like Borges, Stavans, never leaves his precursors unaffected. He understands language(s) as a moving process, which depends on the contemporary mutations of the subject and society within a fluid structure of ever-changing boundaries that transforms language into the articulation of heterogeneous processes. For Stavans, translation is not simply a mirror. For him, it bears a greater resemblance to the broken mirror of the maidservant that Stephen mentions to Buck Mulligan in the opening pages of *Ulysses*. Translation also resembles the burrow of Carroll's White Rabbit,

"Down the Rabit-Hoyo" (Stavans 2021d: 7). It is through this tunnel that we let ourselves fall until we reach the other text, which means an adventure filled with logical paradoxes. These paradoxes invert everything into a new space. Like Alice, our curiosity also leads us to its door though the key can only be obtained if we are brave enough to converse with Dinah, the Cheshire cat. In the pages that follow, we will learn, with Stavans, not only to understand translation as Borges' infinite library, but also to go travel through the looking glass to scrutinize what is on the other side.

Note

1 "Words, words, words taken out of place and mutilated, words from other men—those were the alms left him by the hours and the centuries." Trans. Andrew Hurley, *Collected Ficciones of Jorge Luis Borges*, Penguin, p. 441.

1 Translating in the Postmonolingual era

Between 1993 and 1999, Sebastião Salgado, a Brazilian photographer, created the series *Exodus*. Although many years have passed, the images that he captured in 35 countries are still relevant. Salgado speaks of migrations. His photographs portray the migrations of the Hutus in remote Rwandan jungles as well as those of the migrants that embark in tiny vessels to seek a safer harbour on European shores. Salgado portrays the harsh reality of millions of people, a reality which is as true today as it was over two decades ago.

In contemporary art in all its many manifestations, there are artists whose work focuses on people who are forced to flee their homes and seek shelter in another country. Of course, literature has also described this terrifying situation in works such as *Waiting for the Barbarians* (1904), a poem written by Constantine P. Cavafy in 1898. In 1980, John M. Coetzee used it as inspiration for his novel, also titled *Waiting for the Barbarians* (1980), which depicts this same tragedy. Twenty-five years later, Philip Glass composed an opera of the same name, based on Coetzee's novel.

According to Salman Rushdie, migrations, the displacement of large groups of people, the existence of borders, are "the distinguishing feature of our times" (Rushdie 2003: 425). In the fourth part of *Step across This Line* (2003) of *The Tanner Lectures on Human Values* (Yale 2002), Rushdie reflects on borders, on leaving one's home, one's country, and crossing the boundary to enter a new territory or frontier. He describes the fears, obstacles, and dangers that the decision to migrate brings with it. The border is both literal and metaphorical; it is both moral and amoral. The border shapes us as human beings. As Rushdie so aptly states, we become the frontiers that we cross:

> On the road there were obstacles to overcome, dreadful mountains, fearsome chasms, allegories and challenges. In all quests the voyager is confronted by terrifying guardians of territory, an ogre here, a dragon

DOI: 10.4324/9781003323730-2

there. So far and no farther, the guardian commands. But the voyager must refuse the other's definition of the boundary, must transgress against the limits of what fear prescribes. He steps across that line. The defeat of the ogre is an opening in the self, an increase in what it is possible for the voyager to be [...] The journey creates us. We become the frontiers we cross.

(Rushdie 2003: 414)

The frontier is proof that the human race is divided. We can only survive there if we are docile:

We must be passive, docile. To be otherwise is to be suspect, and at the frontier to come under suspicion is the worst of all possible crimes. We stand at what Graham Greene thought of as the dangerous edge of things. This is where we must present ourselves as simple, as obvious: I am coming home. I am on a business trip. I am visiting my girlfriend. In each case, what we mean when we reduce ourselves to these simple statements is, I'm not anything you need to bother about [...] I am one-dimensional. Truly. I am simple. Let me pass.

(Rushdie 2003: 315, 316, 415, 416)

Rushdie not only refers to physical frontiers but also to invisible ones: "there are frontiers which, though invisible, are more dangerous to cross than the physical kind" (*id.*). Both physical and invisible frontiers require our absolute submissiveness. To survive, we must expunge all our differences and become one-dimensional.

In his reflection, Rushdie looks at a black–and–white photograph from Salgado's *Exodus*. In this snapshot, taken at the Tijuana border, a migrant is running towards Mexico with a Border Patrol car chasing after him at full speed. Rushdie describes the border between the United States and Mexico as a cross between the Great Wall of China and a gulag. According to Rushdie, that fugitive, who has been rejected by all as he runs in terror towards the wall, is the archetypal figure of our era (Bromley 2021).

Step across This Line also includes a short article in support of Edward Said's, *Out of Place*. According to Rushdie, Said

knows everything there is to know about displacement, about rootings and uprootings, about feeling wrong in the world, and it absorbs the reader precisely because such out-of-place experiences lie at or near the heart of what it is to be alive in our jumbled, chaotic times.

Without a doubt, Said is one of the most brilliant intellectuals of our time to reflect on the exodus. In his excellent essay on the experience of exile, he describes our era as "the age of the refugee, the displaced person, mass immigration" (Said 2001: 137–138). Years later, Thomas Nail (2015: 1) forcefully begins his *The Figure of the Migrant,* with the following categorical statement: "The twenty-first century will be the century of the migrant".

In *Vivir adrede* [To live purposely], Mario Benedetti (2007: 105, 106) writes that exile, any exile, is the beginning of another story. This statement undoubtedly summarizes the fate of millions of people in the twentieth and twenty-first centuries. Daily events oblige us to reflect on the fact that contemporaneity is progressively interwoven with the voices of those who live out of place. It is also intricately threaded with those "other" stories that straddle different languages and spaces, stories that are immersed in a diversity that is both conflictive and enriching. *Vivir adrede* is painful, but as Benedetti assures us, it also means discovering and establishing ourselves in our 'interim homelands'.

This chapter explores how the literary work of various writers, especially Ilan Stavans, conveys this situation, thanks to a highly original use of language. My object of study resides in those 'interim homelands', constructed from the stories that greet and welcome us in different languages. This chapter highlights the context in which Stavans' work has emerged by exploring some of the many literary works that reflect our current era of exile and migration. In this situation, translation reveals itself as a phenomenon that is intimately linked to migration and which highlights the complex power relations between languages (Sanchez 2019), given that national identity is reflected in "the struggle over language" (Flores and Yúdice 1990: 59ff).

We currently live in a globalized world in which the only constant is mobility. In fact, as Eva Hoffman (1999: 42) observes, "cross-cultural movement has become the norm rather than the exception". People who have left their places of birth in search of a better life are legion. It is little wonder that in 2015, FundeuRAE[1] chose *refugiado* [refugee] as word of the year. It is a choice that, at the very least, gives us food for thought. Since 2015, the number of people who are "out of place" (to use Said's words) has soared to astronomical proportions. Every day, the media bombard us with harrowing images of refugees seeking shelter. However, after viewing so many, our numbed hearts and minds have become insensitive to them. We have grown so accustomed to this daily tragedy that these images have now lost their ability to stir our consciences and awaken us to the magnitude of the disaster: "images of people whose lives are marked by transience – those whose sense of home has been destroyed by mortar bombs, hazardous crossings, the permanent impermanence of desert camps and the bureaucratic tedium of asylum legislation" (Newns 2020: 1).

Today, thanks to technology, we can be virtually present in various places at the same time. This means that the encounter, mixture, and clash with other cultures are the hallmark of our identity. From a physical and emotional perspective, we live our lives *in between*. And those who have chosen to be transient not of their own will, but for economic or political reasons, are forced to confront and come to terms with borders and walls, which are both physical and metaphorical. All of this happens in a globalized society that proudly claims to have eliminated borders, but who has actually multiplied and reinforced boundaries. This is evident in scenarios from Syria to Tijuana, from Melilla to Calais,

As a result, concepts such as *human rights* and *inclusive citizenship* have been so overused that they have now become virtually meaningless. They exist in stark contrast to others such as *necropolitics* and *necropower*, which designate the capacity to define who matters and who does not, who is disposable and who is not (Mbembe 2016/2019). Although in today's world, it is easy to access what is different, this does not mean that prejudices and difficulties have disappeared. On the contrary, the opposition between *us* and *them* is still very real as is the tendency to define both of these terms by reciprocal negation: the *them* as *not-us*, and the *us* as *not-them* (Bauman 2017).

Exile, a synonym of *displacement*, has always been a constant throughout history. However, during the twentieth and twenty-first centuries, the number of people on the move has skyrocketed. These migrants have been physically and mentally uprooted because of war, violence of all kinds, economic difficulties, and many other problems and catastrophes. In line with Bauman, Nail (2015: 2, 4) links migrations to movement and loss:

> The migrant is not only a figure whose movement results in a certain degree of social expulsion […] The gains of migration are always a risk, while the process itself is always some kind of loss […] The migrant also has its own type of movement that is quite different from the types that define its expulsion. The removal of territorial ownership or access, the loss of the political right to vote or to receive social welfare, the loss of legal status to work or drive.

These important issues have generated a huge quantity of bibliography. Literature, Anthropology, Philosophy, Sociology, and Contemporary Art are just a few of the disciplines that have focused on those who live "not univocally but *contrapuntally*", to use Edward Said's (1993: 59) expression, migrants immersed in more than one culture in the midst of many different voices. For instance, in clear reference to the exodus of the Jewish intelligentsia from Europe, Benhabib's *Exile, Statelessness, and Migration: Playing Chess with History from Hannah Arendt to Isaiah Berlin* (2018) powerfully opens: "In the early decades of the twenty-first century, exile, statelessness, and migration have emerged as universal experiences of humanity" (*ibid.*: xv). Although Benhabib focuses on a different type of migrant than the ones described in these pages, she provides an excellent starting point for our reflections. She expands on her initial statement by showing her deep concern for the unprecedented growth in the number of migrations and displaced people in this millennium. Benhabib's comments, in this book but also in her previous ones (2004), together with, for example, the excellent contributions by Trinh T Minh-h are only a sample of the literature focused on this phenomenon that directly addresses concepts such as citizenship, belonging, global justice, hospitality, politics of difference, governance, cosmopolitanism, security, and border policies, which are analyzed from many different epistemological perspectives:

> Questions arising on the move, at the borders, in the encounter with the other, and when stranger meets with stranger, all tend to intensify around the problem of the *other* foreigner – someone doubly strange, who does not speak or look like the rest of us, being paradoxically at once exotic guest and abhorred enemy.
>
> (Minh-ha 2011: 110)

This is an extremely controversial issue that does not seem to be on its way to being resolved. In a wide range of countries and continents, voices have been raised against migration. Although it is true that from a political and social point of view there is still a call for the existence of borders and the strengthening of existing walls, it is also true that as we enter the third decade of the twenty-first century, the facts and consequences triggered by the voluntary or involuntary movement of millions of people question the idea of a uniform nation-state, which some still wish to maintain. The alternative is a deeply mixed territory in which we have no choice but to rethink our conceptual walls, which are the source of our fears, violence, and oblivion.

As previously mentioned in this chapter, the art world depicts these situations, as can be seen in the reflections of Antoni Muntadas or Guillermo Gómez-Peña (to cite two of the most well-known). Contemporary art is strongly committed to diversity, as evidenced in the flags created to reflect this difference. For example, Gil Mualem-Doron's *The New Union Flag,* which 're-imagines' the Union Jack, is made from fabric designs of colonized communities and ethnic groups throughout the world that contributed to the cultural legacy of what is now Great Britain.

Regarding literature, many contemporary authors represent "the ability to live multiple belongings" (Yildiz 2012: 12). This is the complexity of being more than one, which is a subversion of monochord thinking (Sommer 2003, 2004). However, it is also the ability to live *in between,* to be by translating, and to translate in order to be. It obliges us to reflect on the difference and diversity of spaces, identities, and languages: "what is being said is always being said in another place, in many other places" (Sommer 2003: 293). The interrelation between the different contexts that cohabit the same literary work puts global markets in check in support of the dangerously multilingual polyglot subject (Blommaert 2012):

> This "post" [in postmonolingual] has, in the first place, a temporal dimension: it signifies the period *since* the emergence of monolingualism as dominant paradigm, which first occurred in late eighteenth-century Europe. Such a historicized understanding underscores the radical difference between multilingualism before and after the monolingual paradigm, a difference that previous studies have neglected [...] But besides this temporal dimension, the prefix "post" also has a critical function, where it refers to the opposition to the term that it qualifies and to a potential break with it, as in some notions of postmodernism. In this second sense, "postmonolingual" highlights the struggle *against* the monolingual paradigm.
>
> (Yildiz 2012: 4)

Many of the narratives that emerge in metaphorical or literal border spaces (Arteaga 1997: 11ff) are born of crises of movement and memory. They arise from the interstices and fissures between different territories, histories, and languages, and "cannot be bound by national borders, languages, and literary and critical traditions" (Seyhan 2001: 4). These postmonolingual narratives develop along an "infinitely thin line" (Arteaga 1997: 92) between two languages (Arteaga 1994: 3–4, 1997). This zone, which is literally and metaphorically borderline, includes not only an imposed geographical boundary, but also the psychological, sexual and spiritual (Spoturno 2021: 239 and 241).

These narratives are dislocated stories of fragmented identities and speak of subjectivities, translated and in constant translation, which are the sign of our times (Seyhan 2001: 4). However, earlier authors also used more than one language in their work. For example, to cite only a few examples, the sixteenth-century poems of Mateo Rosas de Oquendo and Sor Juana Inés de la Cruz are characterized by the simultaneous use of Spanish and Nahuatl (Montes Alcalá 2012). Writers such as Beckett, Conrad, and Nabokov used more than one language in their works or wrote in a different language from their mother tongue. As reflected in the work of many scholars, translingualism is both contemporary and ancient, spanning many languages throughout the world. This is evident in Kellman and Lvovich (2022) as well as in their monographic issue of the *L2 Journal* 7, 1, (2015).

Even American literature, which, as Kellman (2020b: 349–350) observes, has always aspired to be monolingual now accepts LOWINUS (Literature of What Is Now the United States) or the study of literature written in languages other than English.

Since literature is generally a territory that reflects social change, there are now quite a few writers who narrate their stories across cultures and languages. What they have in common is that they do not write in their mother tongue. Today's literature has thus become "a post-colonial novel, a de-centred, transnational, inter-lingual, cross-cultural novel" (Rushdie 2000: 57). For example, there are Turkish, Arab, Japanese, Italian, Spanish, and Czech novelists, who write in German. Assia Djebar, Abdelkebir Khatibi, and Amin Maalouf are French writers whose mother tongue is Arabic. Michael Ondaatje, author of *The English Patient* (1992), is a Sri Lankan Dutchman living in Canada whereas modern Italian literature includes writers born in Ethiopia, Morocco, Tunisia, and Senegal.

Undoubtedly, many other authors could also be cited. Though very different, all of them in way or another navigate between two cultures and two or more languages[2]. In fact, perhaps because of its migrant and mobile nature, Jewish literature, which is so close to Ilan Stavans, is an excellent example of translingual literature (Stavans 2021c). Jewish authors such as Sholem Aleichem write in Hebrew and Yiddish; Elias Canetti, in Ladino and German; Ariel Dorman, in Spanish and English; and Joseph Brodsky in Russian and English. There is also Kafka, who wrote in a language that was not his mother tongue. All these writers demonstrate that "translation is not a profession, but a way of being" (Stavans 2021c: 103).

Consequently, literary canons are no longer monolingual but "transnational" in the sense of Appadurai (1996: 146–147). These deterritorialized canons supersede the borders of a single nation or language. Unlike *De Institutione Oratoria* (Lauret 2016), in which Quintilian expresses his distrust of "verba peregrina", pilgrim words that might corrupt the purity of Latin, this rich new literature is replete with migrant or border words that are in continuous translation, transformation, and movement. Insofar as languages belong to and reflect the people that speak them (Pratt 2016), a language in migrant literature is understood as "an active site where the contours of inclusion and exclusion become most visible" (Inghilleri 2017: 2).

One of the many examples is Leila Aboulela, the author of *The Translator*, who was born in Cairo to an Egyptian mother and a Sudanese father. Her childhood was spent in Khartoum, where, despite her family being Muslim, she first attended a Catholic school and then the Khartoum American School. After graduating from the University of Khartoum, she completed her studies at the London School of Economics and later moved to Scotland, where she began to write.

Eva Hoffman, another well-known writer, describes her experiences in exile after migrating from Krakow to settle in Vancouver. In *Lost in Translation,* she describes herself as being "obsessed with words" (Hoffman 1989: 216). She states that Polish is no longer her only language (*ibid.:* 273), and that she regards translation as a kind of a therapy (*ibid.:* 271). Elie Wiesel writes in French, his fifth language after Yiddish, Hebrew, Hungarian, and German. Najat El Hachmi, born in Morocco but raised in Catalonia, writes in Catalan and Spanish, though her novels are spiced with words from the language of her childhood.

Yoko Tawada, a Japanese author who writes in Japanese and German, is building an identity based on traces and superimposed layers. This 'multilingual' network causes her to live in a state of continuous translation. Finally, in *Amour bilingüe,* Abdelkebir Khatibi explains what it means to live between two languages, without belonging to either:

> Language belongs to no one, it belongs to no one and I know nothing about anyone. In my mother tongue, didn't I grow up as an adopted child? From one adoption to another, I thought I was a language's own child [...] This idea imposes itself as I write it: every language should be bilingual! The asymmetry of body and language, of speech and writing –at the threshold of the untranslatable [...] From that moment, the scenario of the doubles was created. One word: now two: it's already a story. Speaking to you in your own language, I am yourself without really being you, fading away in the tracks you leave. Bilingual, I am henceforth free to be entirely so and on my own behalf. Freedom of a happiness which divides me in two, but in order to educate me in thoughts of nothingness.
>
> (Khatibi 1983/1990: 4–5)

The language of the Haitian-American writer, Edwidge Danticat, contains traces of Creole, French, and English, which she uses to recreate the diasporic, transnational, and deterritorialized consciousness and traumatic experiences of Haitians in *Krik? Krat!* (1996), *The Farming of Bones* (1998) or in *Claire of Sea Light* (2013), or her idea of "mobile traditions" and "extra-national spaces," as described in *Breath, Eyes, Memory* (1994). For her, English is her "stepmother tongue":

> I thought of a stepmother tongue in the sense that you have a mother tongue and then an adopted language that you take on because your family circumstances have changed, sometimes not by your own choice. But I don't think of it as something ugly. I've always thought my relationship to language is precarious because in the first part of my

life, I was balancing languages. As I was growing up, we spoke Creole at home, but when you go out, you speak French in the office, at the bank. If you didn't speak French at my school, the teacher would act like she didn't hear what you were saying. French is the socially valid and accepted language, but then the people who speak Creole are not validated and in some way are being told their voice isn't heard. So I've always felt this dichotomy in language anyway.

(Shea and Danticat 1996: 387–388)

This state of affairs invites us to re-examine and rethink the traditional idea that language is linked to national identity: "what happens when the domain of national language is occupied by nonnative writers, writers whose native, mother, home, or community language is not the one they write in?" (Seyhan 2001: 8). This fact, which is so generalized today, makes us wonder what is the point of speaking of pure literary canons (English, French, Spanish literature, etc.), when literary awards such as the Man Booker Prize, National Book Award, and Pulitzer Prize are often won by writers whose mother tongue is not English or who have arrived in a country as migrants or exiles (Walkowitz 2006a, 2006b). This is proof that books no longer exist in a single literary system (Apter 2006: 528) but rather are born in translation (Walkowitz 2015): "Today's writing erupts at unexpected junctures and represents new linkages of disparate and distant places and identities".

All of these writers and many more (Brownlie and Abouddahab 2022; Coste, Kkona, and Pireddu 2022; Kellman and Lvovich 2022; Vidal 2021; Kellman 2020, 2003, 2000; Gilmour 2020; Rose 2020; Tilbe and Khalil 2019; Gilmour and Steinitz 2018; Canagarajah 2017; Doloughan 2017; Moslund 2010; Frank 2008; Courtivron 2003) echo a phenomenon that is not new, but which in today's world is now more visible than ever. At any time and in any place, languages have come to represent considerably more than mere communication. It goes without saying that language contact has always existed. For example, many parts of Africa or India have traditionally been multilingual (Nair 2002), but the right of each individual to speak in the language of their choice is today a basic right (Kohl and Ouyang 2020: 1).

Globalization and the space-time compression that it has engendered have produced multilingual spaces that can be found everywhere and where different languages and identities coexist. Although such coexistence is an evident source of enrichment, it also generates clashes, dislocations, and asymmetries that reveal the extent to which monolingualism has always been a political imposition. This phenomenon is studied in disciplines, ranging from Education and Language Teaching to Sociology, Literature, and Translation Studies. Although it has received various names, current trends in Sociolinguistics refer to this bridging of language boundaries as "translingualism," which recognizes the multiplicity and diversity of contemporary spaces (Li 2018; Lee and Li 2020):

> On the one hand there is the physical movement from one language environment to another. There is also the movement to a different worldview – a different way of interpreting everyday circumstances. The latter can apply even where there is no change in the language spoken.
>
> (Craith 2012: 4)

When these migrant authors use various languages in their work or a language that is not their mother tongue, they are creating plural paths that are often a source of disquiet. They are narrating local stories within that totality from which the universal can be perceived (Mignolo and Walsh 2018: 2). Moreover, the global aligns us with a policy of microspection (Cronin 2012), which permits this multiplicity of trajectories, the simultaneity of the diverse and sometimes (and why not?) contradictory narratives. Their stories speak of "La Migrant Life" (Gómez-Peña 2000: 7ff), and the fear of the other (Gómez-Peña 2000: 61) in the "New World Border" (Gómez-Peña 1996). This is the place inhabited by fragmented, polycentric identities that transcend a single nation and language, identities that traverse dialogic spaces in which the choice of language is not limited to the mere binary oppositions of traditional models (Wilson 2011: 237):

> The effect of mass migrations has been the creation of radically new types of human being: people who root themselves in ideas rather than places, in memories as much as in material things; people who have been obliged to defend themselves—because they are so defined by others—by their otherness; people in whose deepest selves strange fusions occur, unprecedented unions between what they were and where they find themselves. The migrant suspects reality: having experienced several ways of being, he understands their illusory nature. To see things plainly, you have to cross a frontier.
>
> (Rushdie 1992: 124–125)

According to Rushdie, exiled individuals do not find their home in one place but in several, and they express their polycentrism through language. Apart from the inclusion of more than one language, one of the characteristics of these postmonolingual narratives is the use of language in a hybrid, polycentric, and heteroglossic way. Such language use thus becomes a reflection of the borderline identities that create it. Hence, 'strong' languages are deconstructed. This is highlighted in the essay, "English as a language always in translation" (2008) by Alastair Pennycook, who affirms that English no longer functions by itself in a vacuum because it now coexists with other languages and exists in translation: "English always needs to be seen in the context of other languages, or, as I shall argue here, as a language always in translation". In this context, translation "is not so much a method of language teaching or an aspect of comparative literature but rather is a fundamental player on the global stage [...] all communication involves translation" (Pennycook 2008: 40). Languages exist and coexist in translation today in the global and cosmopolitan era, where migrations are a constant. This can often create conflictive situations, as those portrayed in a film as paradigmatic as *The House of Sand and Fog*, based on the novel of the same name by Andre Dubus III.

Even though collective volumes and anthologies on globalization did not initially include the question of language, the relationship between migrations, globalization and language(s) has long been evident (Canagarajah 2017; Pratt 2013). Words are what migrants take with them wherever they go. Of all of their possessions, it is the one thing that they never abandon. And it is their language that allows them to remain in touch with the world they have left behind (Elliott, Gerber, and Sinke 2006).

Although language mixing can initially be a shock, it can also be an enriching experience beyond "English Only" (Pratt 2003, 2012). The coexistence of languages and different accents, and the mixture of semiotic and cultural systems, is a rich context from which one can only derive benefits. It is no wonder that in his 2013 interview with Michel Martin, Ngugi wa Thiong'o referred to contact between languages as the oxygen of civilization. In his 2009 article, "My Life In-Between Languages" (*Translation Studies* 2, 1: 17–21), he asserts that he has always lived in translation, between Gikuyu, his mother tongue, and English, the imposed language. This has inevitably marked his translation and self-translation strategies (Bassnett 2014: 41–43). This "translingual activism" (Pennycook 2008: 43) can be perceived both in the translation and in the readers' reactions to these works and their translations, each of which is the mirror image of the other as well as a reflection of difference and diversity.

Along these same lines, the definition of *translation* proposed by Rey Chow (2014: 65) states that translation should also encompass "a consideration of such illegible and often unconscious elements of languaging as accent, tone, texture, habit, and historicality as well as what is partially remembered, what is erroneous but frequently reiterated, and, ultimately, what remains unsaid and unsayable". It is thus hardly surprising that many of the novels, stories, and poems by postmonolingual authors focus on migrant language and identities, 'strange' accents, the difficulty of speaking 'correctly', and myriad elements that echo emotions and meanings, which, as Chow observes, are said without being said but which still have to be translated.

This is what occurs in *The Buddha in the Attic* by Julie Otsuka; in *The Sound of Language* by Amulya Mallad; in *Unaccustomed Earth* by Jhumpa Lahiri; in "Monday Morning", by Segun Afolab; in "Paper Menagerie", by Ken Liu; in *Foreign Words,* by Vassilis Alexakis; in "Me Talk Pretty One Day", by David Sedaris; and in "No Speak English" from *The House on Mango Street*, where Cisneros portrays a father who ate "Hamandeggs" during his first three months in the United States because it was the only English phrase that he knew.

In Asian literature, there are authors such as Minae Mizumura, who, at the age of 12, immigrated to the United States with her family, but who never felt at home there. Many years later, she managed to return to Japan and to her mother tongue. She is now one of the most widely acclaimed writers in her country with novels such as *An I-Novel,* which encourages diversity in literature and a return to one's native language. She has also authored *The Fall of Language in the Age of English* (Columbia UP, 2017), the English version of her 2008 novel, translated by Mari Yoshihara and Juliet Winters Carpenter, and rewritten for international audiences in collaboration with her. In this book, she stresses the importance of the multiplicity of languages and of diversity in the globalized world of the Internet, where English is fast becoming the sole language. In a world where all languages are supposedly equal, English has become more equal than others.

Many other writers do not aspire to return to their mother tongue, but rather choose to embrace the new culture though without becoming a part of it. Nevertheless, their wish is for both cultures and both languages to coexist and intertwine. For example, the Korean-American author, Cathy Park Hong, uses Korean when writing in English, but even more interestingly, she also subverts English through Korean. What she refers to as "Bad English" appears in *Dance Dance Revolution* (2007), a book of poems that takes place in a fictional city called the Desert. The Desert is a place of constant movement with people from all over the world flowing in and out every second of the day. Its constantly changing language consists of words from over 300 different languages and dialects.

Another excellent example is *Dictée* by Theresa Cha because of her unique use of language, of languages, and images. There is also Xiaolu Gou's reflection on the experience of living in two languages, as conveyed in the hybrid ever-changing language in *A Chinese-English Dictionary for Lovers*. Also relevant is the English used by other well-known Chinese writers such as Amy Tan and Jean Kwok.

Vahni Capildeo, the British poet from Trinidad, concisely describes this situation when she observed that authors today mix languages, and that literature is no longer created only in one language. Instead, modern literature reflects a world that has ceased to be monolingual. In an interview, Capildeo affirms that the English of her childhood in Trinidad is a mirror of the country's history and of its many stories. The English spoken there has words and phrases from West African languages and parts of India, and is also influenced by Spanish, French, Chinese, and Portuguese. Similarly to the contrast of Creole English to 'proper English' in Sam Selvon's *The Lonely Londoners* (1956), Capildeo's experimental poetry also gathers these fragments of multilingual identities, which are always fluid in movement, and characterized by exile, expatriation, and migrations. This is evident in the poem "Five Measures of Expatriation" (2016) from the book of the same name, where the expatriate finds refuge in language. However, this refuge is not in any particular language but rather in one that is always anomalous, foreign, and "accented" (Capildeo 2016: 100).

The United States is another clear example of multilingualism, of the interaction of a multitude of linguistic and cultural trajectories "which are felt also in the many 'impure' linguistic elements" (Shell and Sollors 2000: 8; see also the classic study of Rudin 1996) that surface in the way that different people speak. In these cases and others, such as those of Junot Díaz, Giannina Braschi, and Susana Chávez-Silverman, the author writes in a "weird English" (something that also occurs in other languages such as French or German). This is, in fact, "the new language of literature" (Ch'ien 2015: 4), which reflects the everyday experience of millions of people that inhabit contemporary urban spaces. It is a new English, a "Bad English" (Gilmour 2020) that represents the perspective of those who have been marginalized and silenced for a long time by 'correct' English or Spanish. Consequently, the choice of words by writers such as Chávez-Silverman is much more than an aesthetic choice; it is a political act. This is how she explains her use of Spanish and English at the beginning of *Killer Crónicas: Bilingual Memories* (2004):

> Me han pedido que (me) explique aquí. I mean, que ehplique mi lengua, my use of language. My odd oral, transcultural ortografía. My idioma, 'tis of thee. Bueno, mi lengua … is a hybrid? Nah! Demasiado PoMo, trendy, too Latino Studies (even if it's true). Been there, done that. A verrrrr, mi lengua … es un palimpsesto? Si, eso está mejor. It's a sedimentation of … hmm. OK Para explicar estos mis flights (of fancy), tendría que empezar por decir que soy, it is – my language – cual homing pigeon on acid.
>
> (Chavez-Silverman 2004: xix)

Al punto de que my students aquí en Califas (who have no clue what foreign Hispanopaís I hail from pero saben que I lived recently en Buenos Aires) think that chévere es una palabra argentina! Also, me salen algunos markers de mi niñez en Guadalajara, like fíjate, or sabes qué? Y siempre, signs de mi daily Latinidad, mi Chicana, code-switching life, right here en la cuenca de Los Angeles. Simón, mano. Califas. Orale vato. Carnal, you know?

(Chavez-Silverman 2004: xx)

An me, trotting out my rusty português, worsened by the intervention of Italian, on a Grail-like quest for la colonia brasileira que olí en esa mujer en Tigre ... Time and again ensasché my pathetic little patch-work speech: "Estou procurAndo uma colOnia brasilEira ..." Y me sacaban cheap, high-alcohol "deo-colonias".

(Chávez-Silverman 2004: 113)

Translingual authors of the postmonolingual era do not write in English but rather in one of the "Englishes" (Pennycook 2017, 2010, 2007). This is the case of many African writers (e.g., Amos Tutuola's nonstandard English and Saro-Wiwa's "rotten English" in *Sozaboy*). It is a way of catering to multiple loyalties and linguistic communities (Ch'ien 2004: 248) as reflected in the transforma-tion and deconstruction of the dominant language through the hybridization of its spelling and syntax The modification of the 'correct' accent underlines the social and political implications of using a language steeped in a history of colonization (Ch'ien 2004: 54) and becomes a useful tool for keeping local (hi)stories alive in those "linguistic borders at the checkpoint" (Apter 2013: 3).

Because of the "weird" or "rotten" use of the dominant language, the monolingual reader can either conceive it as incorrect usage or decide to interpret this creativity as variety and richness (Doloughan 2017: 2). The con-cept of 'error' is thus viewed as a way to play with language and position one-self politically by accepting difference (Sommer 2004). However, it is also a way to "interrupt the self-sufficiencies of 'mono' cultures" (Simon 2012: 1).

This is why Emily Apter (2006: xi) states that "[m]ixed tongues contest the imperium of global English". In fact, her concept of "zone", following Pratt's (1992) influential "contact zone", is a kind of encounter and inter-relation that can become a space of violence but also a *topos* that facili-tates the exploration of difference by forcing us to leave behind the known familiar space as well as our mother tongue; Apter's zone describes a broad intellectual topography that is not the property of any one nation but

a zone of critical engagement that connects the "I" and the "n" of transLation and transNation. The common root "trans" operates as a connecting port of translational transnationalism. The zone, in my ascription, has designated sites that are "in-translation," that is to say, belonging to no single, discrete language or single medium of communication.

(Apter 2006: 5, 6))

Indeed, by mixing languages, translingual writers interweave viewpoints and worldviews so that the reader is compelled "to grapple with partial fluency, register the arrogance of U.S. monolingualism, and invent strategies for incorporating the several languages, geographies, and audiences in which they get their start" (Walkowitz 2015: 42). In these deeply metalinguistic works, language is an instrument of power, a way of opposing what has been previously established. Languages are a reflection of living in between, on the border, divided, and translated:

Living in two languages, between languages, or in the overlap of two languages? What is it like to write in a language that is not the language in which you were raised? To create in words other than those of your earliest memories, so far from the sounds of home and childhood and origin? To speak and write in a language other than the one that you once believed held the seamless connection between words and things? Do you constantly translate yourself, constantly switch, shift, alternate not just vocabulary and syntax but consciousness and feelings?

(De Courtivron 2009: 1)

The language of the postmonolingual era is composed of layers. It is a palimpsest created with words that have lived not one but many lives, and which thus tell many stories. These words are polyphonic because if one knows how to listen, they echo the myriad voices of hybrid, dislocated, and impure identities. Their extraordinary richness allows us to see the plurality of worlds and the otherness of the real. These hybrid languages force us to reflect on what it signifies to speak of a nation when one has no home. They cause us to understand what it means to speak of translation when one no longer has a mother tongue and how identity is affected by the loss of one's birthplace. The question is,

Will new makers, maps and split terms accurately describe the conditions of the nomads, migrants, and exiles caught between borders and national definitions? Can one think about a culture in which there are no centers but only borders? How would such a situation change our definition of translation?

(Gentzler 2008: 145)

The words that we come to us are loaded down with diverse and assorted baggage. Their meanings are impregnated with a heterogenous legacy that has been passed down from generation to generation. This inheritance is filled with crevices, gaps, and forking paths along which so many messages thread their way, messages that are neither seen nor heard, but even so, still waiting to be heard. This is the case of *Loosing My Espanish* by H. G. Carrillo (2004), which mixes English and Cuban Spanish. This is precisely why Rosario Ferré's poem in *Duelo del lenguaje* warns that *un beso* is not *a kiss*, and why in *How the García Girls Lost Their Accent*, Julia Alvarez writes that a *mom* is not a *mami*. Language has no real synonyms because words evoke their many past lives.

A language is many languages, insofar as each contains a plurality of cultures and ways of life. The hybridization of language enriches us with its constant movement between cultures, with the possibility of liberating the outgoing and incoming traces, the back-and-forths of words that are also our own:

> Las de ida trazan el camino de los que se fueron, por hambre, por miedo o por las dudas. Las de vuelta dibujan la senda de la nostalgia o del desconsuelo. Las de ida son más hondas, más profundas, resultado de muchas cavilaciones. Las de vuelta son más íntimas, besadas por descalzos.[3]
>
> (Benedetti 2007: 121)

Wanderwords or the 'verba peregrina' so reviled by Quintilian (Lauret 2016) are redolent with the fragrance of all the contexts in which they have been used, and with the scent of all the crossroads, universes, and transactions that they have managed to survive. They inhabit beyond the monotonous monochord discourse of monolingualism, on the other side of the looking glass where the combination of letters is infinite and all melodies possible.

In the postmonolingual era, words are more alive than ever. They are linguistic entities that flow, but always carrying sediment from the spaces that they previously inhabited. This melange that words display is also a tangle of the wrinkles, folds, and imprints that have engendered them. As reflected in the language of Ilan Stavans, there are times when the entropic disorder and paradoxes of contradictory texts exhaust the limits of a dictionary because they bring us closer to voices full of possibilities, in continuous movement, like existence itself:

> Las palabras que oímos desde niños, que escuchamos a nuestros abuelos, que leemos y acariciamos, son cerezas anudadas siempre a otras, y

aunque las separemos con un leve tirón de nuestros dedos mantendrán el sabor de sus vecinas, nos enriquecerán la boca con la savia que han compartido y que se han disputado ... las palabras tienen su propio inconsciente y pueden ser también psicoanalizadas ... Las palabras tienen, pues, un poder oculto por cuanto evocan. Su historia forma parte de su significado pero queda escondida a menudo para la inteligencia. Y por eso seducen. Y esa capacidad de seducción no reside en su función gramatical (verbos, sustantivos, adverbios, adjetivos ... todos por igual pueden compartir esa fuerza) ni en el significado que se parecía a simple vista, a simple oído, sino en el valor latente de su sonido y de su historia.

(Grijelmo 2000: 18–19, 29)[4]

The words we will listen to in the following pages of this book are woven with multi-coloured threads. In the same way as in one of the seven Borgesian nights, where the mirror meets the labyrinth. As these textures are penetrated, they cause us to enter the deepest regions of ourselves through the other. Once inside, the "verba peregrina" remind us that we live in a translated cosmopolitan global world that travels back and forth between languages and cultures beyond monolingualism.

Stavans' (2021: x) literature is "a window to life", where any point can connect with any other, and any voice with any other. Each word is a library of Babel because it contains an infinite number of variations and multiple possibilities of meaning. As in the garden of forking paths, these words capture moments with an infinite number of possible outcomes. According to Stavans, in one of his TED Talks, as one moment is followed by another, each possibility gives rise to a new series of divergent futures.

The true meaning of a word is never found in dictionaries, but arises from the connotations that slowly emerge from the word's multiple interstices and crevices. Meaning is a compendium of the many layers, scars, and (hi)stories that comprise each palimpsestic word. The fascinating meanings that seep through a word's fissures are halos of implications and resonances that invite us to question the meaning of our different worlds and identities, which are necessarily plural.

We thus reach a narrative of changing directions, created from linear multiplicities. This narrative is beyond binary relations between signs. Instead it is closer to the Aleph that contains all other points. It is a narrative made of counterpoints, a fugue full of deterritorializations. As if it were a Borgesian universe, each word can be decomposed into an indefinite and perhaps infinite number of hexagonal galleries.

Notes

1 The FundéuRAE is a non-profit organization founded in February 2005 in Madrid, Spain. The foundation was created in collaboration with the Royal Spanish Academy and under the Department of Urgent Spanish of Agencia EFE.

2 Examples include Meena Alexander, Ariel Dorfman, Junot Díaz, Richard Rodriguez, Esmeralda Santiago, Julia Alvarez, Susana Chávez-Silverman, Gianna Braschi, Jhumpa Lahiri, Elie Wiesel, Emine Sevgi Özdamar, Najat El Hachmi, Gao Xingjian, Milan Kundera, Alain Mabanckou, Abbas Khider, Suketu Mehta, Yoko Tawada, W. G. Sebald, and so many others.

3 Outgoing words trace the path of those who departed because of hunger, fear, or doubt. Returning words trace the path of nostalgia or sorrow. Outgoing words are deeper, more profound, the result of much pondering, whereas words that come back to us are more intimate, kissed by barefoot people [our translation].

4 The words that we hear as children, that we listen to from our grandparents, that we read and caress, are cherries always entwined with others. Even if we separate them with a slight tug of our fingers, the taste of the others will linger on them; they will enrich our mouth with the sap they have shared and struggled for ... words have their own unconscious and can also be psychoanalyzed ... Words then have a hidden power because of what they evoke. Their history is part of their meaning but is often hidden from intelligence. And that is why they seduce. This capacity of seduction does not reside in their grammatical function (verbs, nouns, adverbs, adjectives ... all have the same power) or in the meaning that appeared at first sight or hearing, but rather in the latent value of their sound and their history [our translation].

2 Stavans' multiple identities

It is in this literary context shown in the first chapter where I wish to situate Ilan Stavans' work. In a hybrid territory where languages converge to become one heterogeneous, impure, and diverse language. This language, capable of interweaving the stories of lives that are lived in translation, is the language chosen by Ilan Stavans, Jewish-Mexican-American academic, professor, and translator. A prolific writer, he has published more than 40 books and over 70 edited volumes, such as *The Norton Anthology of Latino Literature, Isaac Bashevis Singer: Collected Stories,* and *The Poetry of Pablo Neruda,* not to mention a vast number of translations as well as countless articles. He is also the publisher of Restless Books, where translation and the need to give a voice to subalterns are the basic principles upon which this publishing house was founded. As professor of Latino and Latin American culture at Amherst College, he defines himself as "a philologist" (Stavans 2021b: 92). He has received a multitude of awards and recognitions, such as the Guggenheim Fellowship, the International Latino Book Award, and the Jewish Book Award. Translated into 20 languages, Stavans' work has also been adapted for stage and screen.

The list of his merits is endless. However, my aim here is to focus on Ilan Stavans as one of the most outstanding representatives of the cross-fertilization of languages and a major exponent of the continuous coexistence of cultures and its resulting hybridization, as rich as it is enriching. Stavans' multifaceted, hybrid identity is precisely why he became a translator. From the moment he immigrated to the United States in 1985, he confesses to being fascinated by translation because of his obsession with the lexicon and its relationship with life. His passion for translation is evident in all of his work, as well as his keen interest in translingualism and hybridization. All of this is vividly reflected in his thought-provoking autobiographical account, published at the end of *The Inveterate Dreamer* (2001), significantly titled "Lost in Translation".

DOI: 10.4324/9781003323730-3

In our hybrid society, we are mestizos. According to Doris Sommer (2004: 19), each one of us is more than one: "How is one to identify, when one is more than one?" These words can be applied to Stavans, who states that he feels different depending on the language that he is speaking (Stavans to Tong 2021): "By virtue of the cross-fertilization defining the world in its entirety, we're all mestizos now", and this is "a state of mind" (Stavans 2013: 36, 37). In his case, being a mestizo is reflected in "la lengua fresca" [fresh language], which is not just language but a way of being, feeling, and dreaming. It is "the interface between *el español* and English, the juxtaposition of ways of being and thinking and dreaming through speech" (Augenbraum and Stavans 2006: xiv). Stavans believes that travelling between languages is as necessary as travelling between identities, and he gives the following advice: "with eyes wide open, venture into unforeseen territory, make connections, and learn different languages" (Stavans 2001: xi). Speaking several languages inevitably means decentring the self:

> To cross the linguistic border implies that you decenter your voice. The border crosser develops two or more voices. This is often the experience of Mexican writers who come to the United States. We develop different speaking selves that speak for different aspects of our identity [...] Working in different languages creates different levels of complicity. When we speak in English, we are the Other. Spanish is for us the language of translation.
>
> (Gómez-Peña in Fusco 1995: 153)

Stavans wanders among words, which are always borrowed words. Like Walter Benjamin's *flâneur* (2950/2006: 53), he loiters among syllables, languages, cultures, and his different selves, always aware that losing one's way is preceded by a learning process. In her introduction to *One-Way Street*, Susan Sontag (Benjamin 1955/1978: 10) recalls that Benjamin describes cities and life with metaphors "of maps and diagrams, memories and dreams, labyrinths and arcades". In my opinion, Stavans also sees life through this same lens. He deeply admires Benjamin, and in *The Inveterate Dreamer* (2001: 190]) he describes him as a "polymath that begs to be approached like a jigsaw puzzle". In the same way as Benjamin, Stavans prefers the fragment, the crevice, the building still under construction, and the kaleidoscopic. Like Benjamin's interpreter in *One-Way Street*, he also uses different fragments not so much to reproduce as to discover other worlds that interact with extremely diverse materials. Like Benjamin, he is fascinated by these scraps and shards that capriciously interrelate with each other in new and unexpected ways.

Like Cervantes' Don Quixote, Stavans is a dreamer, as evidenced in his preface to *Don Quixote: The Novel and the World* (2017). He would also like to wander in the same way as his hero, whose madness according to some (absolute sanity according to others) is actually a way of understanding existence and dealing with the very real unreasonableness of so many. As Frederick Aldama observes in Kevane's (2019) volume, Don Quixote is a major influence on Stavans. Their multiple identities inevitably cause both Don Quixote and Stavans to be regarded as foreigners, "*Un extranjero*, once a Jew always a Jew" (Stavans 2002: 214), always on a journey "*Un* Walker in Nuyol" (Galasso and Scaramella 2019: 15–22).

In his brilliant volume of poems about the wall that Trump expected the Mexicans to pay for, Stavans reflects on all of the concepts mentioned thus far. In that place *in-between*

Places
are
sites
where
fantasy
meets
recognition.

(Stavans 2018b: 5)

And as in the border described by Rushdie, where the gatekeepers encourage docility, here too there are gatekeepers who remind the migrant that the good side is not for him to enter:

"Can
I
get
out?"
asks
the man.
"Out?"
wonders
the
gatekeeper.
"You
mean
in?"
"No,"
responds

the
man.
"Out
of
the
kingdom."
The
gatekeeper
laughs:
"The
kingdom
starts
on
other side,
but
that
side
is
not for you,
at
least
not now."

(Stavans 2018b: 17)

And when the migrant asks how he can get to the other side, how he can
finally come to deserve to enter that other place, the answer could not be
clearer:

"You
must
earn
your
place
in
it."
"How?"
asks
the
man.
"By
always
staying

on
this
side,"
answers
the
Gatekeeper.

(Stavans 2018b: 18)

To be two or more at the same time, to feel oneself between two worlds, to be one as well as the other. To be, in essence, translated. That is why Ilan Stavans is a translated translator:

Paradise
is
now
made
of
halves:
two
doors,
two
desks,
two
Twos

(Stavans 2018b: 23)

The language used by Stavans represents millions of displaced people and reflects this multiplicity of selves:

r
u
are
TÚ ...
Y
tú
eres
lumps,
various
and
unformed,
every
piece

playing,
at
every
second,
su
propio
juego.
And
el
jugo
del
juego
is
proof
that
—¡sorpresa!—
no
hay
diferencia
entre
us
y
ourselves
o
between
nosotros
and
los otros.

(Stavans 2018b: 36–37)

The words of Stavans are *verba peregrina*, wander words, because they cross borders. Unlike Quintilian's aversion for foreign terms, Stavans' language reflects a fascination with difference. His words do not represent single but rather plural identities. They show that the voice that speaks is not one but many:

humans
are
aliens
to themselves.

(Stavans 2018b: 6)

Like Borges, Stavans is fascinated by angles, corners, edges, nooks and crannies. This is perhaps the reason why he loves libraries, those spaces that each of us subjectively organizes to suit ourselves. That is why he asserts in *Dictionary Days* (2005) that the way in which each of us arranges the books in our library speaks volumes about the way we are.

Like Borges, he is attracted to masks, because they are what ultimately unveil the truth (Stavans and Villoro 2014: 147–148). In Stavans' case, the mask as a concept related to identity is a topic that would fill the pages of an entire volume. Though evidently beyond the scope of this study, the notion of mask is highly significant because it portrays a restless, fragmented, polyphonic, and fertile identity, an identity avid for knowledge and always open to the multiplicity of existence.

This is evident in Stavans' use of heteronyms not only in his writing, but also in his translations. Heteronyms reside in a transition zone between reality and fiction. They refer to someone who participates in a strange game in which the creation causes the creator to disappear. The singularity of the author's presence stems from the singularity of his absence. Thus, both authorship and originality become blurred and diffuse, something particularly relevant in the case of Stavans. The masks of heteronomy appear in spaces that are neither homogeneous nor unidirectional. Instead, they emerge in a contradictory and slippery universe. Heteronomy compels us to ask ourselves whether it is the writer who creates and constructs the texts or, conversely, whether it is the texts that create and construct the writer, particularly since the author's name is an unstable signifier that gives rise to multiple interpretations.

Ilan Stavans has published novels, short stories, and translations under other names. Rather than pseudonyms, these names are masks that have their own biographies and titles. They are identities with their own personalities that perform a task with strategies different from Stavans'. In some cases, they have even developed critical theories about it. Although Stavans does not speak publicly about this dimension of his literary production, it is still a fascinating aspect of his work. It is reminiscent of authors such as Fernando Pessoa and his relationship with Alberto Caeiro, Ricardo Reis, and Alvaro de Campos, *inter alia*. But it also makes me think of Francis Picabia, a free-spirited, versatile painter who never ceased to reinvent himself throughout his life. It is little wonder that in 1922, he affirmed that our heads are round so our thoughts can change direction. In that sense, his "transparencies" and masks refer to human beings who would doubtlessly appeal to Stavans because they are dual identities, multiple and intermingled, never univocal.

Precisely because they create masks and multiple personalities, Stavans is also interested in digital spaces and networks that he calls "asocial": "social media in reality should be called *asocial* media: the age of sharing is also the age of minimizing others into misinformed soundbites" (Stavans in Vidal and Stavans 2022: 102). In books such as *I Love My Selfie* (2017), he relates selfies to translation, and links self-translation to self-portraits, from Rembrandt to Mapplethorpe and Ana Mendieta, passing through Magritte and van Gogh. Regarding Rembrandt's almost 100 self-portraits, he observes that each portray the same man yet also a different one, given that the self-translated self changes in space and over time. The self-portraits of Courbet and van Gogh are self-portraits of their mind. In the case of van Gogh, pop art has taken his self-portraits and recreated them in diverse ways (Stavans 2017: 101). Today, their equivalent would be *selfies* and *cellfies*, which speak volumes of contemporary identities:

> Selfies, hence, are approximations of the self. They are a business card for an emotionally attuned world. They promise smiles, happiness, and engagement. In delivering these ingredients, they shape mass taste. Selfies can't stay still; they need to be constantly disseminated, navigating the globe, posted all over for others to endorse with a two-thumbs-up. A selfie taken but stored isn't the real thing; a real selfie needs to be distributed through social media [...] In short, the selfie is performance achieved though overstatement [...] The self, apparently, is made of multiple masks, which is the way it projects itself to the world. For our self isn't a unity but a multiplicity.
>
> (Stavans 2017: 4, 7)

Selfies, like memes, are palimpsests; they are the new identities. "Memes are palimpsests, translating and translating artefacts created by layers of meaning. Memes are snippets of knowledge that carry, in their DNA, a vast cultural cosmos that viewers must decode first" (Stavans in Vidal and Stavans 2022: 99). Memes are translated cultural units composed of many layers and overlapping stories, which dilutes the idea of origin, the trace of an original author. They are multimodal palimpsests that reflect twenty-first-century identities and which Stavans likens to the Altamira cave paintings and hand grenades that distort and unsettle. They tell stories in the voices of many authors and in the voice of none:

> memes are snippets of knowledge that carry, in their DNA, a vast cultural cosmos that viewers must decode first. This mechanism isn't unlike what takes place in parody: for the audience to appreciate the parodic message, it needs to appreciate what is being parodied. Think of *Don Quixote*. Most readers today have never read Amadís de Gaul, Tirant lo Blanc, or other chivalry novelist. Yet entering Cervantes' book, they immediately recognize how Don Quixote is an attempt at ridiculing them. Likewise with memes: upon receiving a meme that

reconfigures a scene of *The Wizard of Oz*, viewers first recognize this 1939 classic film. Creators and recipients must share a common culture for the meme to be effective. But memes include another dimension: they are anonymous. In that sense, to me they are closer to folklore than to art: they are uncredited mechanical reproductions that, while created by an individual, are a product of the collective spirit seeking to give meaning, though the debris produced by internet communication, to the epistemological perplexity of a particular moment.

Memes are Borgesian rewritings that enrich the original with added meaning:

> memes are Menardian: just as Pierre Menard rewrites *Don Quixote* by recontextualizing it—the same exact words acquire an altogether different meaning once they are repeated—the meme extracts an epistemic unit of knowledge from its context and inserts it in another but does something more: it adds to its original meaning by inserting a caustic element in it that turns the original on its head.
>
> (Stavans in Vidal and Stavans 2022)

Neither memes nor selfies are original but rather second originals. They are masks or layers of multiple identities:

> Selfies are palimpsests, too; they are curated, instant, ephemeral versions of the self. Like memes, they exist by creating a community of those who are included—the sender of the selfie chooses its recipients—and also those who are excluded. The difference between "selfie" and "cellfie", and even between these two spellings and a third one, "selfy", is essential: one highlights the self, another the cell phone and the third the monetary transaction engaged by the photograph that is being shared. To me selfies are marketable versions of who we are; they reduce us to a convenient profile, the equivalent of a meme. In fact, selfies (notice my choice of spelling) are often intervened by the sender or someone else, de facto becoming memes. That intervention might be a way of beautifying the picture; or it might be an aggression, a way of demeaning it. In any case, they are similar to translation in that they refashion a real object in subjective ways, thus modifying its meaning. You could call this "demeaning", since by changing the meaning, the meme causes a loss which might involve respect. The translation gives a different kind of respect to the original.

Stavans' multiple and palimpsestic personality is what compels him to constantly doubt and to question everything (Stavans and Villoro 2014:

67). Contradiction, debate, and perpetual metamorphosis keep him intellectually alive. Hence, in *Knowledge and Censorship* (2008: 102), he writes that his life is as entropic as his library, and in his conversations with Raúl Zurita, *Saber morir* (2014), he describes life as a series of unanswered questions.

It is impossible for an identity that is always on the move to confine words, imprisoning them in a dictionary. Mario Benedetti (2007: 177) never trusted dictionaries, because when words enter them, "las pobres están perdidas. Si la palabra está sola, al aire libre, se levanta su significado, dice algo, lo sostiene. Pero cuando entra en el diccionario, la muchedumbre de significados lo asfixia".[1] Stavans is also obsessed with language, which is why he never stops comparing and contrasting words. He collects dictionaries just as he collects *Quixotes*, which is reminiscent of the first part of Cervantes' novel, when the priest and barber make forays into Don Quixote's library. From a different perspective, it also recalls Walter Benjamin's story about unpacking his library, in which he describes his passion for collecting books. Benjamin reflects on the relationship between the collector and the objects in his collection, and on the significance and value of the activity of collecting rather than of the collection itself.

According to Irene Vallejo (2019/2021: 40), every library is a journey, and every book, a passport without an expiration date. In that journey, Borges' Library of Babel, the library of all books, is a haunting labyrinth composed of identical hexagonal galleries connected by staircases and staffed with imperfect librarians. The Library of Babel not only houses all books and languages but also the chronicle of their death. It contains both the true catalogue and the false catalogues. And since its inhabitants barely speak two languages and their time is finite, it is very unlikely that they will locate the book they are looking for in this labyrinth of tunnels.

In a recent publication, Stavans (2021b: 92ff) shows that dictionaries continue to fascinate him. Dictionaries sometimes explore one language, sometimes two or more. Because language is a living organism in constant movement, Stavans is against prescriptive dictionaries, which are authoritarian and set down rules. Language resists confinement and immobilization in the absolute. Words are always inexact, and their meanings infinite and always mutable. This is an excellent description of Spanglish, a language Stavans uses both in his academic writings and translations.

In a subsequent article, Stavans focuses on the *Diccionario de autoridades* (1726–1739). Once again he reminds us that dictionaries are much more than a mere compendium of words. They are a reflection of the identities and societies in which they have been constructed. Accordingly, Stavans (2021e: 1) understands the *Diccionario de autoridades* as "a window to appreciate the impact of Enlightenment ideas in Spain, it also showcases some of the country's most entrenched phobias". It is a prescriptive and colonialist work, which does not take into account other varieties of Spanish, and consequently defines words such as *maya* as a girl who wants to marry a Mayan. The entries for *judío, castizo,* or *casta* are clear indications of the racist bias of the work. The *Diccionario de autoridades* is that space where language reflects the identity of a nation:

> From its front-matter to the tone of its entries, it is unapologetically furiously jingoistic: no matter what, its agenda is to prove that the Spanish language is splendorous, i.e., as capable of depth and complexity as Italian and French. In other words, an inferiority complex palpitates at the core of the project. This isn't surprising. Spanish civilization is built around *el qué dirán*, the tyranny of an outsider's perspective, the way appearances at times override substance. The persecution of Jewish who had converted to Catholicism, known as conversos, as well as heretics, sexual and other deviants by the Holy Office of the Inquisition established a merciless division between the public and private realms. *Autoridades* is a prime example of that imbalance.
>
> (Stavans 2021e: 4)

The *Diccionario de autoridades* endeavours to polish and preserve a language so that it will not change and become 'impure':

> Unmistakably, the idea of Spanish as a pure language is utopian. Needless to say, no languages are truly "pure"; borrowings and other signs of what pedants call pollution are an inevitable feature of being active and in constant dialogue with other linguistic codes.
>
> (Stavans 2021e: 7)

Today we are beginning to understand, albeit gradually, that, fortunately, there are no pure languages. However, according to Stavans, the Academy has still not accepted certain evident realities:

> *Autoridades* records foreign influence on the Spanish language but insistently discriminates against it, suggesting it adulterates Spanish. Not surprisingly, the RAE, without fully abandoning the motto, has chosen a different, even opposing route: the slogan Unidad en la diversidad, "unity in diversity". At least nominally, it represents an effort at being inclusive and wide-ranging, recognizing that the plurality of Spanishes in the Americas, for instance, cannot be subsumed to the normative approach of the Iberian variety. This approach is rather deceitful, though. Behind it is a bias that keeps Spain, illusorily, as the

gravitation center of a civilization increasingly fractured, not to say regionalized.

(Stavans 2021e: 8)

There are countless examples that support the previous statement, such as the cases of domestication as a translation strategy (Marín 2022) in cinema, television, and literature, not to mention the justified anger of Alfonso Cuarón when Netflix subtitled *Roma* in Peninsular Spanish instead of Mexican Spanish.

Stavans' use of language reflects his ever-shifting identity, which transcends the mere coexistence of two languages and is thus a particularly complex and fascinating case. A multiple, heteroglossic, and fragmented identity is a common trait among hybrid writers. In *Imaginary Homelands*, Rushdie (1992: 10–11) describes this identity as a broken mirror, but views it as something positive:

> when the Indian writer who writes from outside India tries to reflect that world, he is obliged to deal in broken mirrors, some of whose fragments have been irretrievably lost. But there is a paradox here. The broken mirror may actually be as valuable as the one which is supposedly unflawed.

Fragments help us to remember the past, but also to face the future:

> The shards of memory acquired greater status, greater resonance, because they were *remains;* fragmentation made trivial things seem like symbols, and the mundane acquired numinous qualities. There is an obvious parallel here with archaeology. The broken pots of antiquity, from which the past can sometimes, but always provisionally, be reconstructed, are exciting to discover, even if they are pieces of the most quotidian objects.
>
> It may be argued that the past is a country from which we have all emigrated, that its loss is part of our common humanity. Which seems to me self-evidently true; but I suggest that the writer who is out-of-country and even out-of-language may experience this loss in an intensified form. It is made more concrete for him by the physical fact of discontinuity, of his present being in a different place from his past, of his being "elsewhere" [...] The broken glass is not merely a mirror of nostalgia. It is also, I believe, a useful tool with which to work in the present.

(Rushdie 1992: 12)

In my opinion, Stavans shares these reflections. His fragmented identity, his changed surname that almost no one can pronounce, and his always out-of-place personalities, *el güerito* and *el ruso*, are reflected in the four languages that he uses:

> I was educated in (into) four idioms: Spanish, Yiddish, Hebrew, and English. Spanish was the public venue; Hebrew was a channel toward Zionism and not toward the sacredness of the synagogue; Yiddish symbolized the Holocaust and past struggles of the Eastern European labor movement; and English was the entrance door to redemption: the United States [...] A polyglot, of course, has as many loyalties as homes.
>
> (en Kellman 2003: 114)

Indeed, Stavans, like all translingual writers, has many homes. As Edwidge Danticat (in Ahmad 2019: 12) states in his introduction to *The Penguin Book of Migration Literature*, migrant literature makes us reflect on what that home is:

> Is home the place where we are born, where [...] our umbilical cords are buried? Or is home the place we die, where we are buried? Or is home the place where we toil in between? The place to which we've sacrificed our youth, our strength, the place to which we have given the best years of our lives? Some of us are born speaking one language and will die speaking another. We are seeds in one soil and weeds in another. We don't always get to decide where we call home. Many times it is others who decide, gatekeepers, immigration officers, border guards.

In this context, the identities of migrants are constructed in movement during their travels between unstable territories, which they map with languages that are ever changing:

> The lexical definition implies that maps are intrinsically unstable, changing according to human will. Consequently, the impact of topography on culture is changeable, adapting to circumstance. Add to it the mutating nature of the environment. The identity that emerges is nothing if not fluid.
>
> (Stavans 2020c: 10)

Ilan Stavans' use of language(s) reflects his multiple identities. His work is the contemporary territory of our times that lies between interim homelands, the one(s) he describes so well in *A Most Imperfect Union: A Contrarian History of the United States* (2014). Moreover, Stavans' work is a postmonolingual territory where language is a reflection of so many other things, and which obliges us to re-examine those conceptual walls that are the source of our fears, violence, and forgetfulness. In fact, Stavans (2021c: 92, 102) links the history of Jewish literature to translingualism, translation, and self-translation.

In *Minima Moralia* (1951), Theodor Adorno warns that morality is not feeling at home when we inhabit the place where we theoretically belong. It is this same sense of morality that accompanies us as we enter Stavans' work. Also present is Homi Bhabha's concept of "unhomely" (1994), a subversive space that appears *inbetween*, a space that is always in transit, and estranged from official discourse. This space is what leads to constantly question our surroundings, those that Cortázar referred to in "Del cuento breve y sus alrededores" [Of the short story and its surroundings].

As a translator, academic, professor, and editor *inter alia*, Stavans creates with his writing, with his translations, and with his displaced originals. Immersed as he is in so many cultures and languages, and in the midst of different voices, he is always thinking about his surroundings: "Language purity is only of concern to those who believe that certain syntactic rules must be maintained. Truth is, language exists in constant change. And miscegenation is an essential linguistic feature" (Stavans 2020a: 14).

Like Borges, Stavans is fascinated by duplicates. Obsessed with mirrors, crevices, nooks and crannies, his identity is a labyrinth of forking gardens. It resembles his "Xerox Man" (1998), a story published in *The Disappearance* (2006), a Borgesian reflection on originality. In this story, Staflovich states that the world is a copy of a lost original. For that reason, nothing in it is authentic, and everything is really a copy of a copy. It is hardly a coincidence that in *The Inveterate Dreamer* (2001: 262), Stavans similarly describes himself as "a copy, an instant replay, a shadow, an imposter. Everything is an echo. To live is to plagiarize, to imitate, to steal". And, in his preface to *Selected Translations, 2000-2020*, he affirms that he is a translated identity, without an original: "I live in translation without an original" (Stavans 2021a: xvi).

Stavans constructs his identities, both the original identities and the translated ones. These identities are intertwined in territories and languages that overlap, and are configured in a continuous state of literal and metaphorical translation. Once again, this highlights the fact that Stavans is a translator in constant translation. In *On Borrowed Words* (2002: 250), he confesses, "Without language I am nobody". In his conversation with Richard Rodriguez, when Rodriguez asks him what it means to switch from one language to another, from Yiddish to Spanish or to Hebrew or English, he answers that each language corresponds to a certain experience and to a certain identity. This makes Stavans a kaleidoscopic being, who is constructed through discourses and reflected in the languages that he uses. This leads him to wonder not so much about *being*, but about the process of *becoming*:

> You know, sometimes I have the feeling I'm not one but two, three, four people. Is there an *original* person? An essence? I'm not altogether sure, for without language I am nobody. Language makes us able to fit into a context. And what is there to be found in the interstices between contexts? Not silence, Richard—oh, no. Something far less compelling: pure kitsch.
>
> (Stavans 2002: 250)

Like other contemporary identities, his identity is far from simple especially since it emerges from interaction and dialogue with collective experiences: "hyphenated identities become natural in a multiethnic society" (Stavans 1995: 17). Both separately and together, his are postmonolingual identities that are constantly translating themselves because they are created with and differently from the Other in an ongoing process that has no end:

> Mexican-American, and (in my case) Jewish-Mexican-American. We are a part of this country, yet separate from it; we're a part of the collective American we, but also proud owners of the fragmented American *I*. Our heritage is complex and sometimes confusing, but then so is the history of this nation we've come to call "home".
>
> (Stavans 2014: xv)

Today, cultural purity is nothing more than a nostalgic fantasy (Fusco 1995: 26), an absurd notion (Bhabha 1996: 53) of the dominant culture that leads to the creation of static symbolic representations. However, these representations are potentially a double-edged sword. Even though it is true that they foment efforts to control cultural difference through the imposition of inflexible models of diversity, at the same time, they also offer the opportunity to transform the stereotypes that result from that control.

In this sense, our existence can only be created through a relationship with the Other, which is necessarily on the border of the homogeneous, outside the hierarchies between spaces and languages, and distanced from the familiar. It is necessary for us to venture outside that comfort zone where it is simpler to silence that which is different, and where we can accommodate ourselves in the space that we believe we have always deserved. This space is so deceptively inviting because it also represents the values and customs that society holds dear. Nevertheless, the drawback to living in this admittedly comfortable space is that an existence within its boundaries inevitably condemns us to ostracism, to monolingual monologue, and to forgetting the richness of opening ourselves to difference.

This means that we must deal with the construction of a monolithic image of the Other (Spivak 1993), created with the precepts of the most hierarchical version of binary representation. The Other is presented to us in its most stereotyped version in order to maintain symbolic and social order (Hall 1997/2003: 258), as opposed to the normative and universalist stance in function of which political and cultural judgments of the latter are formed. Fortunately, there are also discursive spaces such as those offered by Stavans, where each word is neither universal nor homogeneous but "liminal", because each is a rich source of cultural difference (Bhabha 1990: 209).

Stavans' identity is multiple because he speaks many languages, and these languages have shaped him and given him form. Stavans is made up of palimpsestic words laden with memories. Nevertheless, these words are not entirely his own, but are borrowed, passed on to him by those who used them before. Each word has layers, scars that reflect the places where he has been. They reflect his desire to situate himself beyond the homogeneous and uniform fruit of the Lotus-eaters. And for this reason, each of his words is in constant dialogue with its stories, its past, and its echoes and resonances. Concisely put, Stavans is language. Since his language reflects its surroundings, in his work, postmonolingualism is the norm rather than the exception. Each of Stavans' words is a palimpsest of what has been and a project of what will be. Even though each word must be preserved, it must also be pushed to the limit so that language never stands still but becomes a living being in constant movement.

From his postmonolingualism, Stavans is in favour of understanding difference as the shape of the world that surrounds us. Difference is also what lies within each of us. Since all of us are immersed in that linguistic diversity, Stavans would doubtlessly agree that "we are all translators now, whenever we speak to each other—but also whenever we ponder what we justly, but to a large extent putatively, perceive as our own thoughts" (Bauman 1999: 50).

The polycentric scenario of interrelationships and multiple identities of Stavans' work illustrates that monolingualism is much more than a quantitative term referring to the presence of a single language: "Monolinguals are imprisoned in a single-channeled existence" (Stavans 2008: 92). Monolingualism is a principle that has structured modern life, empires, and institutions, and has imposed a hierarchy of languages and of those who speak them. As result, in today's world, Herder's idea of the nation-state has given way to Benedict Anderson's imaginary communities, where language is crucial to the construction (or non-construction) of polycentric, hybrid, and dynamic identities.

Indeed, the relationship between language and identity posited by the monolingual paradigm provides a sense of belonging and reaffirms our belief in a simple uncomplicated narrative of our true origins, and of a univocal, self-contained, and final identity. However, this vision has little or no correspondence to reality. This is the case of the multitudes of people whose mother tongue is a space of limiting and suffocating alienation, even a state of violence and social abjection that blocks the possibility of the multiple and the desire to discover the different (Yildiz 2012). In his essay, "We Are the Clarion: An Immigrant Manifesto", written for the exhibition *My America: Immigrant & Refugee Writers Today*, in The American Writers Museum in Chicago, Stavans states:

> There is no America without outsiders. Call us pilgrims, slaves, refugees, exiles, immigrants, even tourists -we all, directly or indirectly, come from somewhere else. As a nation, the glue tying is together is the shared sense of destiny we nurture and the conviction that somehow this place is different, unlike any other, even exceptional, and that here we may finally breath free. We trade in reinvention. What we were is not who we are and who we will be. It starts with our language [...] English is the nation's dominant language but thanks to immigrants, all other languages (Chinese, Swahili, Bengali, Arabic, Italian, Gaelic ... even Latin) are here too, through nostalgia and as an effort to trace our roots [...] Immigrants are the thermometer that announces the health of a language. The moment we become proficient in English in America, we feel we belong. Yet, our proficiency is stagnant. Willingly or otherwise, we keep a transaction with our original tongues. Look at how American immigrant writers are restless, innovative, pioneering: O. E. Rølvaag, Isaac Bashevis Singer, Vladimir Nabokov, Felipe Alfau, Lucette Lagnado, Jamaica Kincaid, Jhumpa Lahiri, and Edwidge Danticat. They turn English upside down and inside out; they also season it with their original spices into a gorgeous polyglot stew [...] we immigrant writers have something to prove; that something is that America is an unfinished project.

Precisely for this reason, Stavans (2013: 8) harshly criticizes the Peninsular Spanish translations of Latin American authors:

> they have an Iberian imprimatur. This makes them stilted, artificial for scores of readers on this side of the Atlantic. What's worse: to have a good book in a bad translation or not to have it translated altogether? Frankly, I'm frequently torn between these two options, and often opt for the latter. Latino writers also used to be translated in Spain, until

many of us put a halt to the travesty. Now we choose our translators or else we translate the books ourselves.

Translation speaks volumes of the identity of the translator and the person for whom he/she is translating. "Studying *el español* is not about starting from scratch but about regaining what has been lost" (Stavans 2020a: xii). In such cases, translation is a key strategy: "considerations of translation in Latino Studies can lead to a more complex understanding of the work of translators and multilingual works in general" (Stavans 2020a: xviii).

Because of this plural identity and the movement that characterizes it, Stavans believes that the mother tongue is not a homogeneous whole but rather a conglomerate of differential elements that, contrary to the dogma of the traditional monolingual paradigm, are distributed in and through many languages: "an illegitimate language is exactly what I seek" (Stavans 2002: 88). The consequences of this new conception of the mother tongue are significant since it reconfigures Stavans' identity, which signifies that he no longer writes in the singular. His work reflects the context of millions of people who live in a language that is not their own. Or rather, they live in several languages that they regard as their own because they are nomads like he is. They are thus languages always translated, secondary multilingual originals:

> To write is to make sense of confusion in and around [...] I am a copy, an instant replay, a shadow, an impostor. Everything is an echo. To live is to plagiarize, to imitate, to steal. I have always had the feeling of living somebody else's life.
>
> (Stavans in Kellman 2003: 122)

It is hardly accidental that life for Stavans is a journey, a quest in continuous movement. *Reclaiming Travel* (2015), written with Joshua Ellison, is very revealing. The introduction titled "Restlessness" begins as follows: "We are creatures in motion, of motion". In other words, we are creatures on an endless quest. Unlike plants, we are not subject to the earth, but quite the opposite. The history of humanity is a long sequence of comings and goings, back-and-forths, rootings, and uprootings. Since this journey can be physical or mental, one can travel with a book or with a translation. An excellent example can be found in *Selected Translations 2000-2020* (2021), which takes us from Guatemala to Venezuela, Colombia, Argentina, Mexico, Chile, or Peru, from Portugal, Spain, or Switzerland to Russia.

Stavans is well aware that a journey can have either an outward or inward destination. We can feel adrift inside or outside of ourselves, and sometimes both. Like translating, travelling involves not only a change of space but also a change of language and environment, and this means being in contact with the Other. Travelling is a way of approaching the different and coming nearer to it. The journey that Stavans decided to undertake was doubly complex: "The journey, I foresaw, would be twice as difficult, for somewhere along the line I had made the conscious decision to find my voice in a language and habitat not my own" (Stavans 2002: 7).

Travelling does not mean staying in the same place, as the Queen of Hearts warns Alice. It means travelling to translate (oneself), and translating in order to travel. Travelling is a way to deconstruct our own language and to come into contact with the language of others. It is a kind of nomadism, a way to access difference. Interestingly, until the sixteenth century, *journey* did not signify leaving a point of departure to arrive at a specific destination. Instead, it only referred to the beginning of a lengthy trip. As Susan Sontag said in "The World as India" (2003), translating means to circulate, to transport, to disseminate, to explain, and to make (more) accessible. It signifies choosing rather than simply seeking equivalents, which, of course, raises ethical questions. In fact, Sontag asserts that literary translation is above all an ethical task.

Travelling identities are translating identities. Both are related to the creation and deconstruction of representations that are central to the construction and maintenance or the destabilization of the political and cultural hierarchies of a society. This obliges us to consider these two activities in local historical and geographical terms, and not within the context of supposedly universal, neutral, and immovable models. Consequently, crucial questions that arise are how the images created by the traveller influence the ideological construction of identity and difference, and what role do travellers and their narratives play in historical phenomena such as colonialism and the construction of empires. Other questions relate to the role of the wandering translator in the subversion of power when voice and visibility are given to minorities, and, finally, there is the issue of who travels, for what purpose, and with what itinerary. It is necessary to ask ourselves about the social consequences of this and the traces that it leaves in the textual fabric of the culture that receives the translation. As a result, *travel* cannot be regarded as a neutral term devoid of controversy (Polezzi 2006: 171), since the traces of cultural stereotypes and prejudices towards other cultures often emerge from the stories of such travellers.

Stavans' constant journey through and with languages causes us to constantly question ourselves and our surroundings. Through the languages and translations that shape his multiple identities, he allows us to discover, not the landscapes, but rather the traces that such stories have left in them. This type of multilingual journey allows us to discover, not one world, but many worlds that open up for us scrutinize and explore. We can thus feel the difference, the Otherness, always knowing that we are foreigners because all of us are foreign.

This journey can also be seen as an adventure, a search for that space outside reality. This is similar to what Julio Cortázar and Carol Dunlop (1986) did in *Los autonautas de la cosmopista*, an account of the couple's extended expedition along the autoroute from Paris to Marseille. It is an intertext composed of photographs, maps and diagrams, travel diaries, apocryphal letters, stories, drawings of Carol's children, and references to narratives and great explorers (from Cook to Cousteau). In short, this is a kaleidoscope, inspired by Paul Blackburn, Cortázar's friend and translator, in which the *paraderos* [stopovers] that open the door to the other reality are more important than the final destination.

Following Jakobson, Michael Cronin (2000: 9ff) classifies journeys as intralinguistic, interlinguistic, or intersemiotic. He observes, quite rightly, that intralinguistic journeys are the most similar to translation because they entail communication between human beings and the continuous representation and rewriting of different situations. In many cases, language by itself is often insufficient.

Translating allows us to be in two places at the same time, and to be two or more people while still being one. The wandering translator is a metaphor of globalization, of diasporas and exiles, and of the global and local, when neither the mother country nor the place of arrival are simple or univocal concepts. On the contrary, they are related to the never-neutral construction of representations based on supposedly universal models, insofar as the stories of translating travellers and travelling translators often bear the traces of cultural stereotypes and prejudices towards other cultures. That is why,

> to write is, of course, to travel. It is to enter a space, a zone, a territory [...] everywhere characterised by movement: the passage of words, the caravan of thought [...] Here to write (and read) does not necessarily involve a project intent on "penetrating" the real, to double it and re-cite it, but rather entails an attempt to extend, disrupt and rework it ... writing opens up a space that invites movement, migration, a journey. It involves putting a certain distance between ourselves and the contexts that define our identity. To write, therefore, although seemingly an imperialist gesture, for it is engaged in an attempt to establish a path, a trajectory, a, however limited and transitory, territory and dominion of perception, power and knowledge, can also involve a repudiation of domination and be invoked as a transitory trace.
>
> (Chambers 1994: 10)

This is reminiscent of "Dr. Brodie's Report", a story by Borges, inspired by *Gulliver's Travels*, but also related to the first accounts of the New World such as the diary of Christopher Columbus. In this story which addresses the issue of the relationship with the Other and with difference, Borges once again plays with concepts such as veracity, authorship, and origin. At the beginning he confesses that the story, whose first page is missing, is the Spanish translation of a manuscript that was tucked away in an old edition of the *Thousand and One Nights*. The manuscript is narrated by a certain David Brodie, of whom little is known, and who describes some of the more outlandish tribal practices of the Yahoos (a direct allusion to Swift's Yahoos) though he also recognizes their values and ethics. The report begins by lamenting the difficulty of pronouncing the Yahoo language, and thus highlights the need to domesticate and reterritorialize that language. "Brodie's Report" reflects on the Other, on the prejudices of anthropologists, travellers, and translators in regard to foreignness, and on the strategies used to construct discourse about the different.

Whether or not we emerge from the journey unscathed depends on us since there are many ways of travelling. For example, Ulysses, Marco Polo, El Cid, Lazarillo, Don Quixote, Shackleton, Kurtz, Kerouac, and Marco Stanley Fogg of Auster's *Moon Palace* each undertook their respective journeys with very different mindsets. We can either not allow ourselves to be changed by the journey, like Robinson Crusoe, and try to transform the Other by forcing him to become like us, or we can let the journey enrich us since the true traveller, the true translator, is always transformed by this experience. As Iain Chambers (1994) observes, migration is an open-ended process, whereas a journey entails movement between two stable positions. When tourists go on a journey, they know their point of departure and their final destination. In contrast, migrants travel more randomly and this is reflected in their language and identity:

> migrancy involves a movement in which neither the points of departure nor those of arrival are immutable or certain. It calls for a dwelling in language, in histories, in identities that are subject to constant mutation. Always in transit, the promise of a homecoming—completing the story, domesticating the detour—becomes an impossibility.
>
> (Chambers 1994: 5)

Precisely because it cannot be reduced to a mere essentialist binarism, the migrant's journey involves territorializations, deterritorializations, and reterritorializations, insofar as his territory is Deleuzian (Deleuze 1980/1987), and not a Euclidean or Kantian space with geometric coordinates. When migrants territorialize, they make the space their own, and

it becomes their home. In contrast, deterritorialization implies transformation, and reterritorialization involves the sedimentation of the new terri-
toriality in a structure that, paradoxically, will be forever provisional. As
Homi Bhabha (1994: 320) pointed out many years ago, the migrant is in
a constant state of uprooting, which is a nomadic, transnational state of
transcultural fluidity. The migrant's journey is thus rhizomatic, disharmoni-
ous, ever-spreading, forever in-between, multiple, and polycentric. In this
sense, Stavans is very clear that true translation consists in being a traveller
and not a tourist (Stavans 2015) because a journey always involves travelling towards our multiple self:

> The ultimate paradox of travel is that it can be return, escape, and search
> at the same time. We travel to free ourselves from the environments and
> expectations that feel too limiting, too constrictive. But those who are
> deeply compelled to travel are also looking to find a place in the world
> that feels more like home, where we can be both more completely our-
> selves and also less alone. We might never find such a place. It's a
> promise that stays with us and keeps us moving.
>
> (Stavans and Ellison 2015: 145)

Stavans would doubtlessly agree with Stuart Hall, who states that each person's identity is shaped by what he or she lacks. In other words, identity
is made up of what the Other brings, an idea that is crucial to bear in mind
before setting out on a journey. In his essay "Who Needs Identity" (1996),
Hall distinguishes between naturalistic and discursive conceptions of identity, opting for the latter, which conceives identification as a construction, a
process that is never completed. The concept of identity does not denote a
stable, unchanging core or a collective, true self hidden within many other
selves that have a shared ancestry. On the contrary, Hall insists that identities are never unified; they become increasingly kaleidoscopic and multiple,
and are constructed through different discourses, practices, and positions
that are as overlapping as they are antagonistic. The concept of identity
does not refer to a stable core of the self, but rather to a fragmentation that
is reflected in the language used by those who are between two cultures.

For this reason, the debate on identity must be situated within the specific historical events of a community, which cause migrants to wonder,
not so much about being, but rather about the process of becoming, not so
much about *roots* but about *routes* or the journey itself. Finally, they ask
themselves how they have been represented by others, and how they should
represent themselves (Hall 1996/2005: 4).

The space they inhabit is not a unitary space, which also configures them
as intercultural subjects. Hence the concept of contact zone that Pratt applies

to travel literature is actually more social than geographical. It also includes the intralinguistic traveller, the awareness of what language and translation mean in any contact between spaces, and the tension between horizontal and vertical journeys. In this context, a horizontal journey is understood as what is conventionally interpreted as travel, the passage from one place to another, whereas a vertical journey is a more complex experience in which the traveller is keenly aware of local stories, archaeology, and folklore. Both modes of travel interact, and thus relate to translation:

> The sensitivity to language detail is partly then a function of the inter-action between the two modes of travel. If translation is conceived of primarily as translation into the mother tongue [...] then the translator is [...] an intralingual traveler. S/he must horizontally (going to the different regions, countries where the mother tongue is spoken) and vertically (historical sense of language, awareness of detail of place) explore the complex spread of language. The dilemma for the translator is the eternal dilemma of the travel writer.
>
> (Cronin 2000: 19)

During the journey, the reconstruction of identities stems from an "identity as becoming" rather than from an "identity as being" (Hall 1993: 394). It arises from heterology and hybridization, which is never simply the mixture of previous identities or essences, but the result of constant struggle and change. In no case is it a matter of replacing one identity with another, but rather of clearing the way for diverse and dispersed events, for paradoxes and rhizomes.

To start writing is to begin a journey, and to start a journey is to begin a translation. Writing, travelling and translation are driven by the desire to tell stories, and to accumulate stories about stories. The journey of translation is reminiscent of Italo Calvino's *Si una noche de invierno un viajero*, a novel about a journey, or rather about the journeys that a Reader in the company of another Reader undertakes, over and over again, by writing, guided by the machinations of Ermes Marana, the translator who dreams of a literature made entirely of apocrypha, of false attributions, of imitations, of counter-feits, and of pastiches.

However, the journey and the translation also evoke *The Invisible Cities*, in which Calvino rewrites or translates *The Travels of Marco Polo*, without prioritizing the first text (chronologically speaking) over the second. In fact, it is *The Travels of Marco Polo* that depends on *The Invisible Cities* and not vice versa. As is well known, Marco Polo is not the author of his travels, but rather a certain Rustigielo who writes the account at Polo's request while they are both in a prison in Genoa (at least according to the Prologue). In *The Invisible Cities*, Marco Polo weaves tale after tale of the cities he has visited to an ageing Kubla Khan, interspersed with "objectively" written conversations or dialogues between the emperor and Polo. Thus, spaces blend, and meaning emerges from the crevices between the two books.

Stavans is thus one of Calvino's travellers. He takes the languages in which he was born to another location, always bearing in mind that any language is also a migrant. A language is a living organism in constant movement, which never ceases to grow and develop, borrowing from here and there along the way. Life is experienced through language (Stavans 2002: 88). Language determines how we perceive the world (Stavans 2018: 4–5), because each language conveys different emotions:

> Spanish is my right eye, English is my left; Yiddish my background and Hebrew my conscience. Or better, each of the four represents a different set of spectacles (near-sighted, bifocal, night-reading, etc.) through which the universe is seen.
>
> (Stavans 2001: 254)

For that reason, his is a dislocated self:

> I am divided into two hemispheres, two personas. The injury between the two will never heal – but that doesn't scare me – I must find happiness in a divided self.
>
> (Stavans in Kellman 2003: 112)

In his conversation with Juan Villoro, Stavans insists on this idea that he has at least two selves. In constant search of that other, he even dreams of him:

> Yo creo que desde que vivo en inglés, mis sueños han cambiado radicalmente. Son sueños de un trashumante, ni mexicanos ni norteamericanos sino -qué sé yo- sueños liminares, fronterizos, que tienen que ver con el desarraigo, con el desasosiego.
>
> Soy un hombre arraigado en el desarraigo […] Sí sé que a veces me tropiezo en la pronunciación de una palabra o en la construcción de una frase, que tartamudeo en el teléfono, que se me cruzan los idiomas. A decir verdad, me alegra que se crucen. No sé quién inventó la idea de que los idiomas son autosuficientes y deben separarse uno del otro. Yo soy de la opinión contraria: los idiomas se mezclan, se contaminan … Les gusta hacer el amor, jugar a besarse, a tocarse las partes íntimas, a reconocer sus límites.
>
> (Stavans and Villoro 2014: 37–38, 109)[2]

Indeed, like other authors, such as Ariel Dorfman, Stavans is a "wandering bigamist of language", in that he borrows words and gives them back "in a different wonderfully twisted and often funny guise, pawning those words, punning them, stealing them, renting them out, eating them, making love to them and spawning splendidly unrecognizable children" (Dorfman 2003: 34). We are dealing with polygamous authors who give voice to the countless migrants who have globalized their identity today.

Ulrich Beck (1997/2000) calls these people "place polygamists", because they are married to several places and consequently coexist with different values and lifestyles. Their narratives are born during the journey, where, both literally and metaphorically, living spaces become porous and, above all, polyphonic. In these spaces, language cannot be anything other than languages. Monolingualism has no place where cultures intertwine, enrich, and sometimes even clash. As a reflection of life, language is a constant back-and-forth between many voices, different accents, and varying rhythms. Consequently, postmonolingualism is a first step towards bridging barriers and breaking down walls, given the interrelation between language, *topos* and identity, in that constant negotiation between the place of origin and the adopted culture, between "home" and "unhomeliness" (Bhabha 1994: 9), in the here, there and beyond somewhere (Minh-ha 2011: 27).

As I previously stated, Stavans is language, but now it is necessary to revise this statement. Stavans is not language, but languages, and thus he is also several persons and identities. And from his postmonolingualism, he helps us realize that we are all an amalgamation of borrowings and differences because difference is seen very differently, depending on the place from which it is viewed.

Notes

1 The poor words are lost. If the word is alone in the open air, its meaning lifts rises, it says something, and the air sustains it. But when it enters the dictionary, the massive horde of meanings suffocates it [our translation].

2 I believe that since I have been living in English, my dreams have undergone a radical change. They are dreams of a nomad, neither Mexican nor North American, I have no idea. They are more like liminal, border dreams, which have to do with uprooting, with uneasiness. I am a man rooted in uprootedness [...] I do know that sometimes I stumble when I pronounce a word or when I construct a sentence, that I stutter on the phone, that I get my languages mixed up. To tell the truth, I'm glad. I don't know who invented the idea that languages are self-sufficient and should be separated from each other. I believe just the opposite: languages mix, contaminate each other ... They like to make love, to play at kissing, at intimately touching each other's private parts, at acknowledging their limits (Stavans and Villoro 2014: 37–38, 109) [our translation].

3   The *verba peregrina* of Ilan Stavans

Not surprisingly, Stavans' plural identity(ies) has/have resulted in a hybrid literary work that thrives in a translingual context (Kellman 2000, 2003, 2020), in which contemporary literature simultaneously speaks of different worlds in a wide variety of languages and cultures. This chapter focuses on the language of Ilan Stavans, a language that is never written in the singular. For Stavans, language is always languages.

In the preface of *Selected Translations, 2000–2020*, Stavans vividly describes not only what language is for him but also what it signifies for millions of people today. Languages are more than words, and our words are always borrowed. They not only carry their past with them but also reveal our future, because language is a living thing, which is always on the move. Our words are marked by all the places where they have previously dwelt and which have inevitably shaped them. Each word holds stories, traces, scents, and flavours. Words contain the DNA of previous civilizations, and convey ways of seeing and understanding life. For this reason, they allow us to communicate with our contemporaries as well as our precursors. That is why our words, and everyone's words, are borrowed words:

> For me it is harder to think that I was born in Mexico than to say that I was born into Yiddish and Spanish. Languages are more than a lexicon; they contain the DNA of entire civilizations. The words we use aren't really ours; we borrow them, using them to communicate not only with our contemporaries but with those who preceded us and those who will follow us. It is our responsibility to safeguard them while we also push them onto new heights. And, obviously, while creating new words, for no living language is static.
>
> (Stavans 2021a: xv–xvi)

From this perspective, Stavans, along with other important writers mentioned in the first chapter, represents the millions of people who live in

DOI: 10.4324/9781003323730-4

many languages and exist in continuous translation. The literature of these authors is all the more relevant insofar as it reflects the daily problems and concerns of those who have made rewriting a way of life or who have made it their whole life, a life in translation. As we have seen, current migratory flows have generated a literary polyphonic linguistic reality, in which identity and otherness are constructed in relation to the global and local. This is accomplished through narratives that relate the transnational to translation, thus giving voice to diversity, plural identities, and the plurality of identities (Wilson 2018: 55; Wilson 2021). According to Cronin (2006: 45), "The condition of the migrant is the condition of the translated being". This is also true for many contemporary identities, who are also translated beings, translated identities that do not accept the imposed language and create another one that they use "for their own purposes":

> And I hope all of us share the view that we can't simply use the language in the way the British did; that it needs remaking for our own purposes. Those of us who do use English do so in spite of our ambiguity toward, or perhaps because of that, perhaps because we can find in that linguistic struggle a reflection of other struggles taking place in the real world, struggles between the cultures within ourselves and the influences at work upon our societies. To conquer English may be to complete the process of making ourselves free [...] (The word "translation" comes, etymologically, from the Latin for "bearing across". Having been borne across the world, we are translated men. It is normally supposed that something always gets lost in translation; I cling, obstinately, to the notion that something can also be gained).
>
> (Rushdie 1992: 17)

Chapter 18 of *Art and Anger* is enlightening in this sense, because Stavans dedicates it to "tongue snatchers", who practise "the art of switching from one language to another" (Stavans 1996: 204). In an interview after the publication of this book, he explains how he came to learn Spanglish from a student of his:

> I let him loose – and was immediately taken by envy. His tongue was freakish but free, and his speech was -what? Hermoso, beautiful [...] What was my duty as a teacher: to teach him proper Spanish and English? I was puzzled. Should I have condemned his use of this bastard vehicle of communication? Aren't languages in a constant flux?
>
> (Stavans in De Courtivron 2003: 131)

If Quintilian defended the homogeneous against what he perceived as barbaric and foreign, the hymn to postmonolingualism is, in contrast, recognition of the richness implicit in diversity. This is the context of Stavans' Spanglish, the reflection of a hybrid world that is all the more enriching as it becomes increasingly plural. It is the fertile soil for the seeds of the many *verba peregrina*, which are the subject of the multitude of essays and translations that reveal Stavans' position on key issues such as identity, migrations, and even racism.

> No espeak inglés?
> Just pretend,
> amigo.
> Over there
> not everyone
> speaks
> the language
> Either.

> (Stavans 2018b: 45)

Stavans does not use his words to compose arias but rather to create counterpoint analyses, as proposed by Edward Said in *Culture and Imperialism*. His pentagrams are not those of a symphony. Instead, the musical score created by his words is "an atonal ensemble" whose *finale* is a heterogeneous and polycentric topography:

> we must take into account all sorts of spatial or geographical and rhetorical practices – inflections, limits, constraints, intrusions, inclusions, prohibitions- all of them tending to elucidate a complex and uneven topography.

> (Said 1993: 386)

Spanglish is that polycentric, uneven, multi-layered territory that has overcome binarisms and essentialisms, which are the characteristics of all migrant literature:

> We are not talking about the old comparative and binary approach of retrieving identities (influences) and highlighting differences (nativist essences). Instead, this multicontextual approach is characterized by its alertness toward a multiplicity of simultaneous dimensions. This means that it takes into account historical, geographical, and rhetorical "strategies," thereby revealing a complex and uneven territory—not merely between the authors but also within each author's literary design. The atonality is an effect of the interdependence and overlapping of locally inflected literary experiences across national borders, just as it is an

effect of the migrant author's impurity of double belonging, a configuration that additionally transforms history and geography into new cartographies that are far less stable than before and where new transversal connections intensify.

(Frank 2008: 122)

From this perspective, Spanglish, as a mixture of languages, should always be referred to in the plural. It is a symphony of accents that vary depending on the geographic space. For example, the Spanglish of the U.S.–Mexico border is different from that spoken in other areas of the world:

> The Spanglish of the border is different the Spanglish anywhere else in the United States, Latin America, the Caribbean, and Europe; it is also different from cyber- and social-media Spanglish. It is less settled and more disorganized—in eternal flux. I have studied it over the past few decades. It changes depending on who is passing through, what historical factors are affecting the area, and how the region is being portrayed in the media, among other factors.
>
> (Stavans 2020c: 10)

Spanglish has generated a great deal of controversy (Betti and Enghels in Stavans 2020c: 347–380; Montes-Alcalá 2019: 319ff), and has as many detractors as defenders. In *The New York Times* (1997), Lizette Alvarez described Spanglish as:

> the language of choice for a growing number of Hispanic-Americans who view the hyphen in their heritage as a metaphor for two coexisting worlds [...] It's a phenomenon of being from two cultures. It's perfectly wonderful. I speak English perfectly. I speak Spanish perfectly, and I choose to speak both simultaneously [...] Spanglish has few rules and many variations, but at its most vivid and exuberant, it is an effortless dance between English and Spanish, with the two languages clutched so closely together that at times they actually converge. Phrases and sentences veer back and forth almost unconsciously, as the speaker's intuition grabs the best expressions from either language to sum up a thought. Sometimes entirely new words are coined.
>
> (Alvarez 1997: 1)

Decades after Alvarez's article, Spanglish is now everywhere. It is spoken on the streets, but is also a research focus in literature, art, and sociolinguistics.

In fact, sociolinguistics regards Spanglish as something infinitely more complex than mere code-switching:

> not as two autonomous language systems as has been traditionally the case, but as one linguistic repertoire with features that have been societally constructed as belonging to two separate languages.
>
> (García and Wei 2014: 2)

Spanglish is "translanguaging" if the term is conceived as "the creative and critical deployment of semiotic resources in communication that transcends normative boundaries between named languages" (Lee and Li 2021: 558). Spanglish thus involves the counter-normative language use (Pennycook and Otsuji 2015; Otsuji and Pennycook 2021) that describes power relations between languages and monolingualism as a political imposition:

> The act of Translanguaging creates a social space for the language user by bringing together different dimensions of their personal history, experience, and environment; their attitude, belief, and ideology; their cognitive and physical capacity, into one coordinated and meaningful performance [...] and this Translanguaging Space has its own transformative power because it is forever evolving and combines and generates new identities, values and practices. Translanguaging underscores multilinguals' creativity—their abilities to push and break boundaries between named language and between language varieties, and to flout norms of behaviour including linguistic behaviour, and criticality—the ability to use evidence to question, problematize, and articulate views [...] Translanguaging goes beyond hybridity theory that recognizes the complexity of people's everyday spaces and multiple resources to make sense of the world.
>
> (Li 2018: 15)

From an academic perspective, Spanglish can also be regarded as a means of political and social vindication:

> While some prescriptive linguists, editors, and authorities in education would judge the interference of Spanish in English as a deficit, a postmodern and transcreative approach would validate it as a positively creative innovation in literature. Indeed, the most important contributions of U.S. Latina/o writers to American literature lie not only in the multiple cultural and hybrid subjectivities that they textualize, but also in the new possibilities for metaphors, imagery, syntax, and rhythms that the Spanish subtexts provide literary English. Needless to say, this

transformation is not restricted to the formal sphere, and its political and social implications regarding readership are only now beginning to be discussed. What on the surface appears to be a praxis that signals cultural assimilation may be defined also as a subversive act: that of writing the Self using the tools of the Master and, in the process, transforming those signifiers with the cultural meanings, values, and ideologies of the subordinate sector. Underlying intertextuality clothed in the language of the Other.

(Aparicio 1994: 797)

What Frances Aparicio (2019) calls the "intralatina" generation is one that is proud of its multiplicity and difference, something that leads its members to create a Latino space of belonging. Spanglish is *tropicalization* (Aparicio 1994, 1988), and tropicalization means seeking a polydirectional and multivocal approach to the mainstream politics of representation. *Tropicalizing* means not being afraid of the colonial gaze that essentializes subaltern cultures and privileges the dominant ones (Aparicio and Chávez-Silverman 1997: 14). "Tropicalizing has to do with the transformative power of the subaltern subject" (Aparicio and Chávez-Silverman 1997: 2). According to Stavans (2020c: 5), tropicalism "is a rhythmic (e.g., syncopated), polymorphous response to the binary-modeled Western setting".

Stavans describes Spanglish as an encounter between the Hispanic and Anglo civilizations, but also as "a frame of mind" (Stavans 2008b: x) that reflects society and is thus ubiquitous. Spanglish pertains to the frontier, to movement, and to topography:

The US–Mexico border, because of its fluidity, is an uber-national zone. Topography is turned upside down and inside out in it. That mishmash is perfectly tangible in the languages that converse in the region. Spanglish is only superficially its lingua franca. In truth, Spanglish is a Rubik's-Cube test.

(Stavans 2020c: 5)

In Stavans' opinion, Spanglish is one of the many 'border languages' that exist today:

Franglais, portunhol, hibriya, etc. Among immigrantes están también las "middle-step" lenguas: *Yinglish,* por ejemplo, una mixture de Yiddish y English. Spanglish es una border lengua, as well as una "middle-step" lengua. En verdad no hay un Spanglish sino una amplia variedad: el Spanglish de los Cuban-Americans, called *Cubonics;*

Dominicanish, que usan los Dominican-Americans; *Nuyorrican*, de los Puerto Ricans en New York; Chicano; y así.

(Stavans 2021d: v–vi)

Language says a great deal about us. It betrays our thoughts and feelings; it can reveal our attitude towards languages. It also expresses our openness to the world. The words that we decide to speak, our choice of what we silence, and the ways that we communicate or say what we say are never casual or innocent. That is why in *The Pleasure of the Text*, Barthes (1973/1975) states that meaning is produced not only by linguistics and grammar but, above all, by the myriad elements within each word. According to Barthes, language is an immense halo of implications, of effects, of echoes, of turns, returns, and degrees; words are replete with vibrations and flavours.

These reflections are in line with how Stavans uses language, knowing that every word contains stories, that every word bounces off other words in all directions. Words are "time codes. In their essence, they contain the DNA of the people that created them" (Stavans 2020c). All words communicate; they carry and generate resonances. That is why they all have a place in his universe: "My passion for Spanglish in no way diminished my devotion to Spanish and English. Indeed, I believe in multiple loves" (Stavans in De Courtivron 2003: 145).

The discussion of Stavans' relationship with dictionaries in the previous chapter shows that he believes that the Real Academia Española is a prescriptivist institution, "la patria desmadreadora" (Stavans 2014: xiv), in its normative zeal to ensure the unity of Spanish. From the perspective of postmonolingualism, fragmentation is not a problem but just the opposite:

¿Es el Spanglish una afronta al español? If so, qué bien. Does it represent its demise? De ninguna manera. ¿Debe el inglés preocuparse del amplio número de hablantes, unos cuarenta millones a nivel mundial? A Little.

(Stavans 2020b: 14)[1]

In view of this, Stavans affirms that he is:

un proud Spanglish-parlante, que para mí has a lot to do with being hispano en EE. UU. and also Jewish. Este idioma bastardo es absolutamente democrático: by la gente, for la gente y para la gente. As time goes by, está ordenándose in such a way que se vislumbra ya una standardized sintáxis.

(Stavans 2020a: 14)[2]

Stavans' translation of part of *Don Quixote* comes from his reaction to the superior attitude of peninsular Spanish, as he himself explains in an article:

> During a lecture tour through Orwell's Catalonia in the summer of 2002, I participated in a radio discussion, broadcasted live, on the origins and nature of Spanglish. Among the participants, who were either present or connected by satellite, there was a language purist affiliated to the Real Academia Española de la Lengua Castellana. There was some discussion on the capacity of a language to express emotions and the challenge Spanglish faces in this area. In his diatribe, this *caballero* stated that the mongrel tongue should not be taken seriously until and unless it produced a masterpiece of the caliber of *Don Quixote of La Mancha*, the magnum opus of Iberian letters, published by Cervantes in two parts, the first in 1605 and the second one in 1615. My immediate response was one of agreement. It's too early to say what pattern Spanglish will take in its development, I suggested. While it isn't impossible that in a couple of hundred years such a masterpiece might be composed in a variety of Spanglish unfamiliar to us today, a "translation" of the novel isn't at all impossible, and neither is it improbable.
>
> (Stavans and Charron 2004: 183)

It is this Spanglish that Stavans has studied and translated so extensively from *Don Quixote* to *Hamlet* to *The Little Prince*. In the preface of *Wáchale!* (Stavans 2001), he sums up this mixture very well in the following reflection:

> La muerte de una lengua es acompañada frecuentemente por una letanía de lamentos. El progreso va demasiado rápido, se dice, la gente es alérgica al cambio. Por ejemplo, hubo acaso cerca de 2000 lenguas indígenas en lo que ahora llamamos América Latina, de las cuales quedan ahora solo unas 600. Su desaparición es sin duda trágica.[3]

In contrast, the birth of a new language is ironically greeted with resentment and annoyance, not to mention disbelief.

> El espanglish no es aún un lenguaje en el sentido propio del término. No tiene una gramática estandarizada. Y su ortografía es inestable. Sin embargo, este idioma híbrido es usado por millones de hablantes en las Américas, en especial en los Estados Unidos, que contiene a la segunda concentración de gente de origen hispánico en el planeta. Hay docenas de variedades, no definidas sólo por la extracción nacional

[...] También están formadas por la edad, la raza y la educación del hablante, así como por el momento de llegada como inmigrante. La base del espanglish es a menudo, aunque no siempre, el español. Las tres características más sobresalientes en un hablante es el cambio de códigos (de ida y regreso del castellano al inglés), la traducción simultánea y la formación de neologismos.

(Stavans 2016: 3)[4]

Stavan's *Spanglish: The Making of a New American Language* (2003) was received with both praise and criticism. That *casteyanqui, inglañol*, Saxon slang, bastard Spanish, *gringo papiamento*, and *pachuco caló* that as Stavans himself recounts (De Courtivron 2003: 129), Octavio Paz detested: "neither good nor bad, but abominable" (Stavans 2008b: 64). And not only Paz but other critics, such as Roberto González Echeverría (2003) in *Letras libres* (Stavans 2008b: 116ff) and José Saramago (Stavans in Albin 2009: 210), regard it as the speech of poor illiterate Hispanics who do not know how to express themselves in either of the two languages. Stavans' answer to these criticisms is that these are opinions far removed from the reality of the subalterns and are impoverished visions of those who dwell in an ivory tower:

It isn't spoken only por los pobres, the dispossed. The middle class has embraced it as a chic form of speech, una manera moderna y divertida de hablar. [...] Spanglish, instead, is democratic: de todos y para todos. [...] it is not defined by class, as people in all social trata, from migrant workers to upper class statements like congressmen, TV anchors, comedians, use it regularly.

(Stavans 2003: 20)

This translingual language, "la jerga loca" (Stavans 2003), appears in translations such as *Don Quixote*:[5]

In un placete de La Mancha of which nombre no quiero remembrearme, vivía, not so long ago, uno de esos gentlemen who always tienen una lanza in the rack, una buckler antigua, a skinny caballo y un grayhound para el chase. A cazuela with más beef than mutón, carne choppeada para la dinner, un omelet pa los sábados, lentil pa los viernes, y algún pigeon como delicacy especial pa los domingos, consumían tres cuarers de su income.

El resto lo empleaba en una coat de broadcloth y en soketes de velvetín pa los holidays, with sus slippers pa combinar, while los otros días de la semana él cut a figura de los más finos cloths. Livin with él eran una housekeeper en sus forties, una sobrina not yet twenty y un ladino del field y la marketa que le saddleaba el caballo al gentleman y wieldeaba un hookete pa podear.

El gentleman andaba por allí por los fifty. Era de complexión robusta pero un poco fresco en los bones y una cara leaneada y gaunteada. La gente sabía that él era un early riser y que gustaba mucho huntear. La gente say que su apellido was Quijada or Quesada but acordando with las muchas conjecturas se entiende que era really Quejada. But all this no tiene mucha importancia pa nuestro cuento, providiendo que al cuentarlo no nos separemos pa nada de las verdá.

(Stavans and Augenbraum 2006: 23)

Don Quixote is one of the most translated literary works in the world. It has been translated into more than 140 languages. In fact, it has more than 20 English translations. So Stavans asks why not make a translation into a language spoken by millions of people who live between two languages and two cultures. *El Little Príncipe* and *Alicia's Adventuras en Wonderlandia* are also migrant versions of these works for migrants and a reflection of migrations.

Esta versión de *Alice's Adventures in Wonderland* en Spanglish es el result de years de trabajo. Empezó, without yo knowing it, cuando yo transladé, in 1999, el first capítulo de Part I de *Don Quixote*. Since then, mi interés en esta hybrid lengua, un back-and-forth entre el español and English que es neither español o English, se ha incrementado substantially. Spanglish es un global fenómeno that responde a la unavoidable condición del present: la immigración.

Spanglish is spoken by approximately 50 million people, not only in the United States but throughout the world. Generally speaking, Spanish speakers are bilingual: Spanish and Spanglish, or English and Spanglish. They can even be trilingual: Spanish, English, and Spanglish. Why not give this diasporic nation its own *Alice's Adventures in Wonderlandia*? (Stavans 2021d: v). It is in this *Alicia* that the cat helpfully points out, "In that direction vive el Hatter", and, "waving la otra paw", announces where "vive una March Hare", "both locos". In the face of homogeneous language, Stavans opts for Spanglish, which is as heterogeneous as the lives it reflects:

Basta darse una vuelta por los barrios de La Villita o Pilsen en Chicago o East L.A. en Los Ángeles o caminar por la calle 8 en Miami para darse cuenta de lo enfático, lo permanente y lo heterogéneo que es el espanglish. Digo heterogéneo porque no hay un espanglish sino muchos: el cubonics, el dominicanish, el nuyorrican, el pachuco, y así.

Cada uno tiene su propio metabolismo, su propia idiosincrasia, aunque hay elementos que los unen. Lo mismo puede decirse de las variantes del español en el mundo hispánico.

(Stavans y Villoro 2014: 110)[6]

Translating is not simply a question of dressing a book up in different clothes but one of "repositioning of that book for a new generation" (Stavans 2021b: 19). Thus, the translation of this literature that reflects a generation also reflects the world in which it was born:

> Ours is a universe infused with translations. From the conversation with a long-distance operator, a taxi driver, a tourist, and a newly-arrived immigrant, to the browsing of foreign channels on our cable network, the pleasure of a novel drafted in another language, to the debate on bilingual education and "English Only" and "English First" [...], ours is a universe inundated by translation. Increasingly, it is everywhere you go. Yet we are fixated on the fact that the degree of encounter in translation is dissatisfying, that something is always lost. It surely is, but, as far as I'm concerned, something is also won, so to speak. Who are we when we are translated? Has our self been adulterated, deformed, and reinvented? Might it have been improved, perhaps?
>
> (Stavans in Sokol 2004: 84)

According to Gabriel García Márquez, combatting the despair of being uprooted, Colombian villagers, fleeing floods, plagues, and other natural disasters (but also the desolation caused by endless civil wars), did not forget what was most important to them when they packed their bags. As they were just about to become nomads, they went to the cemetery and dug up the bones of their ancestors to accompany them on their journey into the unknown. They were doubtlessly spurred by the need to defy the fluctuations of time and space, by the illusion of having something of the past to cling to, something permanent that would remain intact in their present, a solid link to memory in a time of devastating change that undoubtedly threatened to fragment their identity (in Dorfman 2003: 29).

In less complicated situations, immigrants do not go so far. They just pack their suitcases with a few photos and other mementos of the past. In more complicated situations, such as those of present-day refugees, not even that. Nothingness is the only thing that accompanies them.

However, in all cases, even in the most dramatic scenarios, the language, their language, always accompanies them, even though that language will be of little use to them in the place of arrival. They will be forced to push it into the background if they want to be accepted in their host country. How to cope with this dual language situation will become one of their worst nightmares.

The frontier represented by language for a people trying to begin life in a new country where everything, (customs, food, people, etc.) is foreign is perhaps one of the highest walls that they will have to climb. But what vital changes does living between two languages force one to come to terms with? What does it signify write in a language that is not the language of your mother, the language of your childhood memories, the language in which the relationships between words and things were first built in your mind and memory?

Stavans, like other contemporary translingual authors, has managed to transform the depressing situation of those who are forced to live in interim homelands into a much more enriching scenario, in which no language, no *verba peregrina*, is renounced. Instead of biasing or dividing, his goal is to interact with and achieve the intersection between languages and worlds. These intersections are not a safeguard from wounds. In fact, sometimes, they even cause them. Nevertheless, any hurt is worth suffering because only pain makes us feel alive.

Stavans' interim homelands are palimpsestic spaces that speak to us with words that accumulate many lives, and with hybrid languages that have been constructed in those intersections populated by stories of change and colliding realities. Nonetheless, they also expose the reverse side of the tapestry of the storytellers, which reveals their innermost selves. And the identities that occupy these hybrid spaces are (multiple) identities also in movement, which influence each other because they perceive a double, triple, polycentric world, and at the same time, they are also perceived in this world. They are identities in continuous transformation, in constant be-being.

In these circumstances, language is undoubtedly one of the first barriers encountered by the inhabitants of these interim homelands. Language is that space where identities are constructed and reconstructed. Postmonolingual speakers like Stavans remind us, with their boundless creativity, that the homogeneity and purity of languages is an ideological construct, and that all languages are social constructions. In the hands of these speakers, words never stand still.

What is fascinating is that Stavans' use of words causes these worlds to interrelate, interact, and leave traces on each other. Because of their power to articulate references, to foment different perspectives of thought, words harbour the seeds of possible discourses, and thus eliminate any possibility of creating walls between sentences. Such walls are a sign of dogmatized thought, which always seeks homogeneity and the comfort of established limits. Stavans' postmonolingual language is a demonstration that we live at the intersections of stories, experiences, languages, and translations. His every word is a dialogue of scripts, and scripts are the source of inexhaustible interrogation. That is also why each melody is a continuous composition and arrangement of different viewpoints, as when the same musical theme is played in different tonalities.

Stavans' words are wander words that travel between cultures and exist in continuous translation. Yet, at the same time, they are constantly translating. They create interferences and nomadic interrelationships, and are always on the move. According to Mary Louise Pratt, being multilingual is more than to be constantly translating; it is to live in more than one language and in constant translation; it is to be caught up in an endless process of "unfolding" (Pratt 2002: 35). In this context, language is a never-ending back-and-forth between contact zones that rub against each other, creak, screech, and even clash with each other. This confirms that the writer has no choice but to go beyond language, and that the condition of the migrant is that of a translated being, who moves from a source language and culture to another target culture. Translation thus takes place in the physical sense of movement but also in a symbolic sense of the shift between one world and another, and between one identity and the other. These identities are never essentialist, never unified, but become increasingly kaleidoscopic and multiple. They are constructed through different discourses, practices, and positions, often as overlapping as they are antagonistic. Stavans' poems, narratives, and translations do not only speak languages; they speak worlds.

The world proposed by Stavans is a palimpsest because his books are as well. They are like notepads on which the traces of the previous sheet can still be perceived on the one underneath. The writing has disappeared yet it still remains. In these works based on his own original, Stavans offers us rewritings that bear the traces of a long journey. As John Berger observes, traces are not only what remains when something has disappeared. They can also be the harbinger of a project, heralding something still to be revealed. Perhaps this is why Roland Barthes insists that *writing* should be an intransitive verb. Stavans' writing certainly is. His writing is a way of living. He lives in writing and through writing by translating life, both literally and metaphorically.

3.1 Nuyol: the space of multiple voices

Place, the space where people speak, or the space that generates a particular way of speaking, is an important concept in the work of translingual authors in general and in Stavans' work in particular. Accordingly, his introductory chapter to *The Oxford Handbook of Latino Studies*, entitled "North-South, East-West: Topographies of Latinidad", is "an invitation to understand not only perspectives but also knowledge as linked to geography" (Stavans 2020: xiii). Furthermore, it is also a reflection on the geographical dimensions of the concept of "Latinidad" that he had already begun in 2011 in his book (with Iván Jaksić) *What is la Hispanidad?* The concept of place is intimately linked to migrations:

> Refugees, exiles, immigrants, and other transients have cognitive maps enabling them to regenerate their sense of place based on their move from one another place. While that move frequently involves suffering, it eventually allows them to become someone new […] *Hispanidad* is an abstract concept encompassing a diverse assortment of people irrigated between two continents and across almost 7.5 million square miles, disjointed by a common language. […] It is a civilization with a loose (e.g., conjectural) sense of geography. That sense projects itself relentlessly, shaping stereotypes defined by two coordinates that strive from the way people perceive their differences.
>
> (Stavans 2020c: 4)

In polycentric cities such as New York, refuge is sought by multitudes of people whose identities become dislocated as they are absorbed into a new *topos*. In multilingual spaces of globalization, customs, and values intermix, and the concepts of belonging and origin are transformed. This gives rise to geocritical readings of identity discourses, because *space* is now *spaces*, while the out-of-place identity always carries the traces of its other origin, which coexists with the new territory. Contemporary spaces are as diverse as their inhabitants, and thus as diverse as their languages. The world today is many worlds; its inhabitants continue to be in movement despite the frontiers and walls that are still being erected today, more or less surreptitiously, in human rights societies. All too often, contemporary cosmopolitan, multilingual, and multicultural cities are not the cities of refuge that Jacques Derrida (1997/2001) so desired.

In a thought-provoking chapter on contemporary cities as translated spaces, spaces in translation, Azade Seyhan talks about Berlin, Los Angeles, and New York as follows:

> "ciudades traducidas", multilingües, multiculturales, que los migrantes han transformado. Son lugares que reflejan el policentrismo contemporáneo y que, en consecuencia, invitan a la reflexión ética: "positioned in the fold of a paradox that represents both the security of home and the inevitability of migration, the city confronts the ethical imperative of settling its inhabitants as it allows for their differences".
>
> (Seyhan 2014: 216)[7]

Seyhan goes on to say that the literature of those who live in translation has used these spaces as representational spaces in which to reflect on linguistic and cultural exchange. In these translated cities, translingual writers use "translation and self-translation to bring to language what they could not say in their own languages or what was censored in their own countries" (Seyhan 2014: 220). The translated city "is not merely an agglomerate of asphalt and concrete and parks and monuments, but a palimpsest of images [...] forms the backdrop for the diasporan's confrontation with the past and the lost home" (Seyhan 2014: 221).

It is in New York that Stavans discovers the mixture of languages: he hears and listens to Spanglish, Franglais, and Chinglish (Stavans in Tong 2021). New York City is a text that communicates. It is a space where the most diverse languages intertwine. New York is one of those places where what architecture refers to as "spatial translation" (Rabourdin 2020; Akcan 2012) comes alive. Like other multilingual cities, with their multiple "linguistic landscapes", here architecture, buildings, and spaces recreate and build a "semiotics of the city" in the sense of Roland Barthes' "Semiology and Urbanism" (1967), where he assures that whoever loves cities also loves signs. Further on, Barthes proposes something with which Stavans would agree. He states that in order to conform a semiotics of the city, it is necessary for there to be many and varied readings. We should never try to completely fill the structure because this would put an end to other interpretations, the number of which should be infinite.

In this sense, Umberto Eco's semiotics of architecture and his collaborations with Venturi are also relevant. This is also directly related to language conceived as a spatial practice in Deleuze and Guattari's *A Thousand Plateaus*, in Lecercle's *The Violence of Language* and in some essays by Heidegger. But the most visual example is that provided by Stillman, a character in Paul Auster's *City of Glass*. In Chapter 8, under the watchful eye of Quinn, the detective writer, Stillman wanders around city. During this apparently aimless journey, his wanderings trace the phrase "Tower of Babel" with, through, and from the streets of New York (Rabourdin 2020, 2016). In Chapter 10, Stillman disappears since he has finally become part of the city. At the beginning of the novel, Auster describes New York as an inexhaustible space in which to get lost, just as we get lost inside each other. New York is that nowhere whose centre is everywhere. It is a fragmented and plural space, which, like any text, is open to multiple interpretations.

In these cases and in others, New York is presented as a multilingual text that reflects many different ways of life. It is a city full of echoes and resonances, as described by Giannina Braschi in en *Yo-Yo Boing!* (1998):

New York es una lata de resonancias y una lata de atardeceres y sonid os-resounding-resounding-resounding.
    Crude is the word, raw.

Como una zanahoria. Una zanahoria cruda.
It's the last great European city. And the first great American city.
And the capital of Puerto Rico.
his city has always been apocalyptic. Since the turn of the century,
when the subways were laid [...] Memory has few landmarks. Wear
it down. Tear it down. Beethoven rolls around Central Park on roll-
erblades and motorcycles, and hes a contemporary of Jackson and
Madonna vis a vis walkmans. Every pair of ears picks its own noise.
The dead are alive, alive and rolling around, like dice in Wall Street.

(Braschi 1998: 129)

Giannina Braschi discusses Spanglish in terms that are both vital and political:

Existe y está vivo—ahora más que nunca. La realidad bilingüe está a
punto de decidir las elecciones en Estados Unidos [...] Spanglish fue
un movimiento cultural que se convirtió en una realidad política. Hoy
en día más de la mitad de los puertorriqueños se han mudado a Estados
Unidos y decidirán las elecciones, junto a los mexicanos y otros inmi-
grantes latinoamericanos que irán a las urnas mañana. Hay dos mov-
imientos en la historia de la colonización: invasión e inmigración. La
emigración es una reacción a una invasión. Emigran porque han sido
invadidos. Se trata de cambiar la perspectiva desde el punto del coloni-
zador al punto de vista del colonizado.

(Braschi in Stavans 2020c: 354)[8]

Braschi is one of the authors who most fervently support the mixing of
languages, as highlighted by Doris Sommer and Alexandra Vega Merino
(1998: 12, 14) in their introduction to *Yo-Yo Boing!* (1998):

Errancy, in this book, is not a problem; it is a way of being that obeys
the mixed signals of complicated contexts [...] from the mirror-image
title that bolts back and forth, from Spanish to English, from one subject position to another (yo and you). Not pendular, not melting to a
middle ground, but bolting from one ground to another in the daily
self-juggling that bilinguals perform with the pride of their agility, with
the richness of excess.

Braschi (1998: 142) defends the multiplicity of languages, cultures, and
lives:

If I respected languages like you do, I wouldn't write at all. El muro de
Berlín fue derribado. Why can't I do the same. Desde la torre de Babel,

las lenguas han sido siempre una forma de divorciarnos del resto de la humanidad. [We] must find ways of breaking distance. I'm not reducing my audience. On the contrary, I'm going to have a bigger audience with the common markets—in Europe—in America. And besides, all languages are dialects that are made to break new grounds. I feel like Dante, Petrarca, and Boccaccio, and I even feel like Garcilaso forging a new language. Saludo al nuevo siglo, el siglo del nuevo lenguaje de América, y le digo adiós a la retórica separatista y a los atavismos.

It is little wonder that Stavans (2020d: xi) is one of Braschi's greatest fans:

I have always visto a Giannina Braschi como mi heroína. And I'm an adicto […] There is something mágico in her juego de palabras, her exploration of tenses, her anxious, uncompromising bilingüismo que ni es de aquí ni es de aquí ni es de allá, ni tiene age ni porvenir, y ser feliz es su color, su identity. Braschi crea una lexicography that is and isn't atrapada en el presente.

We are dealing with writers who create polyphonic texts in constant translation, and who, with their multilingual "linguistic landscapes", transform the city into a postmonolingual space, as observed by Regina Galasso (2019: 1, 2):

thinking about translation and the city is by and large a way of telling the backstories of the cities, texts, and authors that are united by acts of translation […] Translation is the ideal idiom for studying the city because of the rich interpretive space of cultural and historical diversity that it generates.

Stavans acknowledges this (2002: 11, 15). When he arrived in New York, he wanted to lose himself in its streets to read the city: "walking the city, reading it" (Stavans 2002: 11). In this way, he unknowingly situated himself in a new line of research that has generated a fascinating collection of literature (Lee 2021; Jaworski and Li 2020; Simon 2012, 2012; Pennycook and Otsuji 2015), which conceives the city as a text that translates and which translates itself. This is because the city is a book written with many voices and many stories.

For Stavans, New York is that heteroglossic book. It exemplifies Sherry Simon's (2012) dual city, a multilingual city full of "translation sites" (Simon 2019). Stavans' Nuyol is the translingual city where postmonolingual space is transformed through languages that intersect for both aesthetic and political purposes (Simon 2012, 2018; Lee 2021). It is little wonder

that, according to Simon (2012: 1), "[a]ccents, code-switching and translation are to be valued for the ways in which they draw attention to the
complexities of difference, for the ways in which they interrupt the self-sufficiencies of 'mono' cultures". Like Simon, Stavans realizes the importance
of listening to the city. This is why he defines New York as the city where
languages between fraternal strangers intermingle:

> This, surely, is the source of sources, a city of fraternal strangers, of
> cultural sophistication and high civilization, the city of Walt Whitman
> and Federico García Lorca and Henry Roth, where tongues intermin-
> gle to such a degree that a new language seems to be born every other
> second.
>
> (Stavans 2002: 13)

From the very beginning, Stavans sees New York as a polyphonic text that
he absolutely must read (Stavans 2020: 11). However, he is aware that this
will not be an easy task:

> The journey, I foresaw, would be twice as difficult, for somewhere
> along the line I had made the conscious decision to find my voice in a
> language and habitat not my own.
>
> (Stavans 2002: 7)

New York is an enormous multilingual, polyphonic book:

> From the first moment I stepped out into New York, it appeared to me
> like a huge book, a novel-in-progress perhaps, filled with anecdotes,
> with a multilingual poetry impossible to repress.
>
> (Stavans 2002: 11)

He discovers New York as he wanders through the pages of Alfred
Kazin's *A Walker in the City*. According to Regina Galasso (in Kevane
2019), this is something that links Stavans to Alfau. On those streets he
was amazed to hear so many different 'Spanishes' than the one he spoke
in Mexico:

> In what language should I describe este walk in Nuyol? There is a
> Babel of slangs coexisting all around me. It is a Russian roulette: eve-
> rything is lost and won in translation. Yet New Yorkers don't translate.
> They just erupt into the world in whatever tongue they feel most com-
> fortable in.
>
> (Stavans 2018a: 223)

On one of his wanderings in New York, he hears "Esplanglish" for the first time: "It sounds atrocious. Why can't they make up their mind? The constant back-and-forth contaminates everything" (Stavans 2018a: 225). However, among the Latinos in the city, a mixture of Spanish and English is the norm.

Spaces like New York are places where 'minor' languages are gaining ground, or rather where major languages are progressively becoming minor in the sense of Deleuze and Guattari, who, in *Kafka: Toward a Minor Literature*, describe to perfection the global phenomenon of the millions of people who do not live in the language in which they were born:

> How many people today live in a language that is not their own? Or no longer, or not yet, even know their own and now poorly the major language that they are forced to serve? This is the problem of immigrants, and especially of their children, the problem of minorities, the problem of a minor literature, but also a problem for all of us: how to tear a minor literature away from its own language, allowing it to challenge the language and making it follow a sober revolutionary path? How to become a nomad and an immigrant and a gypsy in relation to one's own language?
>
> (Deleuze and Guattari 1975/1986: 19)

The concept of 'minor literature' is taken from an entry in Kafka's diary that has to do with literature written in Yiddish. Deleuze and Guattari claim that it is a literature constructed by a minority in a major language. Minor literature is written in a language that deviates from the standard. It is a political and deterritorialized literature that evokes "the revolutionary conditions for every literature within the heart of what is called great (or established) literature" (Deleuze and Guattari 1975/1986: 18). In this context, the texts are written in a language which is not pure:

> Even when it is unique, a language remains a mixture, a schizophrenic mélange, a Harlequin costume in which very different functions of language and distinct centers of power are played out, blurring what can be said and what can't be said; one function will be played off against the other, all the degrees of territoriality and relative deterritorialization will be played out. Even when major, a language is open to an intensive utilization that makes it take flight along creative lines of escape which, no matter how slowly, no matter how cautiously, can now form an absolute deterritorialization.
>
> (Deleuze and Guattari 1975/1986: 19)

Mil plateaux (capitalisme et schizophrénie) is one of the later works of Deleuze and Guattari that discusses the relationship between major and minor languages. It insists on the need to deterritorialize major languages, especially since the unity of language is fundamentally political:

> The unity of language is fundamentally political. There is no mother tongue, only a power takeover by a dominant language that at times advances along a broad front, and at times swoops down on diverse centers simultaneously ... Must a distinction then be made between two kinds of languages, "high" and "low", major and minor? The first would be defined precisely by the power (*pouvoir*) of constants, the second by the power (*puissance*) of variation.
>
> (Deleuze and Guattari 1980/1987: 101)

Deleuze and Guattari state that it is basically a question of using languages in different ways:

> "Major" and "minor" do not qualify two different languages but rather two usages or functions of languages [...] Minor languages are characterized not by overload and poverty in relation to a standard or major language, but by a sobriety and variation that are like a minor treatment of the standard language, a becoming minor of the major language. The problem is not the distinction between major and minor language; it is one of a becoming. It is a question not of reterritorializing oneself on a dialect or a patois but of deterritorializing the major language [...] Minor languages do not exist in themselves: they exist only in relation to a major language and are also investments of that language for the purpose of making it minor. One must find the minor language [...] on the basis of which one can make one's own major language minor [...] Conquer the major language in order to delineate in it as yet unknown minor languages. Use the minor language to *send the major language racing*.
>
> (*ibid.*: 105)

In contrast to the homogeneity and statism of the 'major' language, the 'minor' language is all about becoming. The ultimate goal is to achieve the becoming-minor of the major language:

> minor languages are not simply sublanguages ... but potential agents of the major language's entering into a becoming-minoritarian of all of its dimensions and elements. We should distinguish between minor languages, the major language, and the becoming-minor of the major

language. Minorities, of course, are objectively definable states, states of language, ethnicity or sex with their own guetto territorialities, but they must also be thought of as seeds, crystals of becoming whose value is to trigger uncontrollable movements and deterritorializations of the mean or majority

(*ibid.*: 106)

In my opinion, Stavans' use of languages exemplifies these philosophical reflections. Without framing it in these terms, Stavans encourages a "rhizomatic" use of language, which is open to mapping, interconnection, in-betweenness, pluralism, and hybridization:

The rhizome is altogether different, a *map and not a tracing*. Make a map, not a tracing [...] The map does not reproduce an unconscious closed in upon itself; it constructs the unconscious. It fosters connections between fields [...] It is itself a part of the rhizome. The map is open and connectable in all its dimensions; it is detachable, reversible, susceptible to constant modification. It can be torn, reversed, adapted to any kind of mounting, reworked by an individual, group or social formation. It can be ... constructed as a political action or as a mediation [...] A map has multiple entryways, as opposed to the tracing, which always come back "to the same".

(Deleuze and Guattari 1980/1987: 12)

Very different from a binary structure, rhizomatic language is deterritorialized, ever-changing, reversible, connectable, and non-hierarchical:

Unlike a structure, which is defined by a set of points and positions, with binary relations between the points and biunivocal relationships between the positions, the rhizome is made only of lines: lines of segmentarity and stratification as its dimensions, and the line of flight or deterritorialization as the maximum dimension after which the multiplicity undergoes metamorphosis, changes in nature [...] unlike tracings, the rhizome pertains to a map that must be produced, constructed, a map that is always detachable, connectable, reversible, modifiable, and has multiple entryways and exits and its own lines of flight. It is tracings that must be put on the map, not the opposite. In contrast to centered (even polycentric) systems with hierarchical modes of communication and preestablished paths, the rhizome is acentered, non-hierarchical, nonsignifying system without a General and without an organizing memory or central automaton, defined solely by a circulation of states.

(Deleuze and Guattari 1980/1987: 21)

The language of so-called 'minor' languages becomes a way of conceptualizing migrant identity. In this context, translation is inescapable, because the identity of these people is marked by translation. For them, translation is a condition *sine qua non* not only for existence but also for survival. In fact, one of the first major obstacles that migrants face is being unable to speak the language. It is at this point that translation intersects with issues such as exile and power asymmetry.

Translating between asymmetrical languages in one direction or the other, from English to Spanish or from Spanish to English, is a very intriguing topic that has many power implications (Sánchez 2019). As Spivak (1999) wrote many years ago, the fact that the subaltern cannot speak makes him even more invisible. His reaction is to trans-create language, beyond any simplistic binarism, as a denunciation of monolingualism. He thus demonstrates "the hability to live multiple belongings" (Yildiz 2012: 12).

Stavans, "an immigrant to the Unaited Estates", author of such important works as *The United States of Mestizo*, uses hybrid language in various translations and even in academic articles. Proponents of language mixing speak of tolerance and diversity. On the opposite side are those who champion "English Only", and who fear that the "true" American identity will be irrevocably lost. To those intent on preserving a monolingual America, Ariel Dorfman (in Stavans 2008b: 119) answers as follows:

> For those who are afraid and claim it can't be done and believe that the United States can only endure if it is monolingual, there's a simple answer. It comes in words that have been heard on the streets of America in recent days, sung and imagined by men and women who crossed deserts and risked everything to live the American dream. In words that the nation's founders and pioneers might have embraced, and that have now become part of the national vocabulary:
>
> *Sí, se puede.*
>
> Yes, we can.

Notes

1 Is Spanglish an affront to Spanish? If so, how cool. Does it represent its demise? No way. Should English be concerned about the vast number of speakers, some 40 million worldwide? A Little [our translation].
2 A proud Spanglish-speaker, which for me has a lot to do with being Hispanic in the USA as well as Jewish. This bastard language is absolutely democratic: of the people, by the people and for the people. As time goes by, it is gradually

becoming more organised, and so a standardized syntax is probably looming on the horizon [our translation].

3 The death of a language is often accompanied by a litany of lamentations. Progress moves too rapidly, they claim. People are allergic to change. For example, there used to be maybe 2,000 indigenous languages in what we now call Latin America. Now only about 600 remain. Their disappearance is undoubtedly tragic [our translation].

4 Spanglish is not yet a language in the proper sense of the term. It has no standardized grammar. And its spelling is still inconsistent. Nevertheless, this hybrid language is used by millions of speakers in the Americas, especially in the United States, which has the second largest Hispanic population on the planet. There are dozens of varieties that are not defined only by national origin [...] They are also shaped by the age, race and the education of the speaker, as well as by his or her time of arrival as an immigrant [our translation].

The basis of Spanglish is often, but not always, Spanish. The three most salient characteristics in a speaker are code-switching (talking back and forth from Spanish to English), simultaneous translation, and the creation of neologisms [our translation].

5 See Villegas (2013) for an interesting analysis of this translation, and Montes-Alcalá (2019: 326) for criticisms of this translation by various authors.

6 One need only take a stroll through the neighbourhoods of La Villita or Pilsen in Chicago or East L.A. in Los Angeles or walk down 8th Street in Miami to realize how emphatic, how permanent, and how heterogeneous Spanglish is. I say heterogeneous because there is not one Spanglish but many: Cubonics, Dominicanish, Nuyorrican, Pachuco, and so on. Each has its own metabolism, its own idiosyncrasies, although there are elements that unite them. The same can be said of the variants of Spanish in the Hispanic world [our translation].

7 Multilingual, multicultural "translated cities" that migrants have transformed into places that reflect contemporary polycentrism and which thus invite an ethical reflection: "positioned in the fold of a paradox that represents both the security of home and the inevitability of migration, the city confronts the ethical imperative of settling its inhabitants as it allows for their differences" [our translation].

8 It exists and it is alive – now more than ever. Bilingual reality is about to decide the U.S. election ... Spanglish is a cultural movement that has now become a political reality. Today more than half of all Puerto Ricans have moved to the United States and will decide the elections, along with Mexicans and other Latin American immigrants who will go to the polls tomorrow. There are two movements in the history of colonization: invasion and immigration. Emigration is a reaction to an invasion. People emigrate because their country has been invaded. It is about changing the perspective from the colonizer's point of view to the point of view of the colonized [our translation].

4 Original translations
Stavans' quest between the second and third original

4.1 A translated life

The many books and articles on Ilan Stavans reveal that he has been translating for over twenty years. Doubtlessly, this is so because in reality, he has been a translator for as long as he can remember because his is a life lived in constant translation. In his case, translating is a strategy for survival. And in the same way as survival, language is also in constant flow. Stavans translates himself and is translated. He has translated from Spanish, Hebrew, French, Portuguese, Russian, and German as well as other languages. He has also translated a wide variety of different authors such as Borges, Neruda, Emily Dickinson, Elizabeth Bishop, Sor Juana Inés de la Cruz, Raúl Zurita, and Cervantes.

Perhaps because he is so many people, so many fragments, being a translator brings him happiness in the sense of Walter Benjamin. In translating, he is "happy to wander as I wonder", like Benjamin's traveller, along Borges' forking paths. And perhaps because he is more than one person, he wonders if he ever had an original self (Stavans 2002: 250). In the prologue to his *Selected Translations, 2000–2020*, Stavans asserts that translation is a form of liberation, insofar as the words in one language become other worlds when they are transfigured in the target language:

> To me, *Selected Translations* is a *carte d'identité*. This is one of my selves, perhaps the most important: I'm a translator. I live through translation and I translate in order to live. I'm an immigrant as well as a descendent of immigrants. Translation and immigration come hand in hand. To me the word "translation" is a synonym of home, or maybe homelessness. When I translate, I'm at home — mind you, a temporary home, never a fixed one. I know some of my homes better than others. What I like about them is that I'm a renter, not an owner. In other words, I'm always in transit. Another way of understanding

DOI: 10.4324/9781003323730-5

translation is being alert to foreignness. I don't like the idea of translation as domestication. For me a text is like a stranger knocking at the door. I make the stranger be comfortable; I create a suitable atmosphere for the stranger to feel acclimated. But the stranger remains a stranger and mine the welcoming hand […] I find *re*reading far more rewarding than reading.

(Galasso and Stavans 2021: n.p.)

Stavans goes on to say that he is a migrant, a condition that he relates directly to translation. Like so many other authors, translation in his case is not a calm and leisurely activity, but "a productive (and sometimes violent) space of the border" that marks "a departure from traditional vertical models in which sense or ideas 'trickle down' from the original (as a source of profound meaning) to translation (as an interpretation toward depth)" Karpinski 2012: 12). In this sense, Stavans' translations deconstruct the hierarchy between the original and secondary language (and culture) and thus turn translation into a transversal activity: "a transversal movement across surfaces that reveals unexpected linkages and genealogies" (Karpinski 2012: 12).

Stavans has not only migrated from one space to another but from one language to another, from Yiddish and Spanish to Hebrew and English, among others:

I'm an immigrant. This is my condition. Immigration is untenable without translation. Translation fosters a kind of immigration. To translate is to survive on day-to-day basis.

I started my life in Yiddish and Spanish interchangeably, then changed to Hebrew, hoping for redemption, and eventually settled in English, with other companions like Ladino saving me along the way. I am ambivalent about the term "mother tongue" to describe my first language, for where are all subsequent ones left? Are they stepmothers? Mistresses? I also don't like describing them as "firsts" because it gives them an unsustainable location. Whatever tongue one is using at the moment is first. For those reasons, I prefer a leveling of fields: all languages — all *my* languages, for that matter- are equal; I love them just the same. All are engaged in giving birth to reality.

(Stavans 2021a: xv)

As a result, like many translingual writers, Stavans does not know for sure which language is his mother tongue. As highlighted in the first chapter, many authors such as Elias Canetti, Emine Sevgi Özdamar, and Ian McEwan, *inter alia*, have also reflected on this issue (François 2017). In fact, the question of mother tongue, or mother tongues, and their relation to identities and cultures, is a constant in these writers. This can be observed in Wendy Lesser's anthology (2004), which collects the reflections of 15 authors (e.g., Ariel Dorfman, Amy Tan, Ngugi wa Thiong'o as well as others), who write in English but whose 'mother' tongue is another language. This is a subject of great interest to Stavans, and is widely discussed in his work (Stavans 2001: 254ff), precisely because he loves all his languages equally. With each language, he creates realities, sensations, emotions, and worlds. If language is "an emblem of belonging" (Craith 2012: x), the situation of migrant hybrid writers makes it clear that their belonging is multiple and that their identity is plural.

Stavans' approach to the act of translation is reminiscent of Walter Benjamin. At the beginning of Benjamin's article on the translator's task, first printed in 1923 as an introduction to a Baudelaire translation, he states that a good translation is not intended as an intermediary text for a receiver who does not understand a certain language, especially since the life of the original reaches its widest scope in translation and is always renewed. Benjamin goes on to say that translation reveals the intimate relationship between languages, which goes beyond the creation of an exact likeness.

In the course of its survival, the original is modified by translation. This is perhaps the most revolutionary Benjamin, and it is certainly what we find in Stavans' translations. Translation is not a sterile equation. As Benjamin observes, all languages complement each other. As an example, he gives *Brot* and *pain*. Even though they are 'synonyms', *Brot* means something different to a German than *pain* to a Frenchman. Languages are incomplete, which is why he sees translation as a way of interpreting what is unique about each one.

Benjamin's theory of translation proposes something different from the mere reproduction of meaning. The aim of Benjamin's translator is not to recompose the broken vessel so that it is exactly the same as before. Fidelity and freedom are not for him antagonistic concepts when translating. The fragments must match one another though they need not be exactly alike. He does not see faithfulness and freedom in translation as antagonistic tendencies.

All of these ideas emerge in the analysis of Stavans' translations. He is evidently in consonance with voices such as Coldiron and other scholars, who do not speak of an original and a translation but of one text and an earlier text. Although in all likelihood, Stavans devotes little time to pondering over contemporary translation theories, it is fascinating to see how he has been able to actively apply those theories in his translations.

Stavans lives a translated life without an original (Stavans 2021). In fact, he claims to have written *On Borrowed Tongues*, "in translation without an original, that is to give my English a variety of accents" (Stavans 2018a: 6). Each chapter is imagined in a different language: "the Yiddish of my paternal grandmother, the Spanish of my childhood, the Hebrew of my ali-yah to Israel, and the English I adopted when settling in New York in the 1980s" (Stavans 2020a: 13). A translation may even be an improvement on the first text (Stavans 2001: 229). As observed by Borges in "On William Beckford's *Vathek*" (1943), translation completes the original.

As in the case of other translingual writers, translingual translation can be a political stance against Standard English or Spanish (Stavans 2001b). In Stavans' second originals such as *Alice's Adventuras in Wonderlandia* or *El Little Prince*, all the voices, all the music, are heard (Pratt 2002: 33). In these texts as well as others, translations are a way of countering the monochrome vision of univocal thought. Translation is "a synonym of transformation, of alteration and movement" (Stavans 1995b: 36). Thus for Stavans, translation symbolizes communication, dialogue, and the encoun-ter between very dissimilar entities. Even though much is lost in translation, all rewriting is an attempt to reach the other. Stavans has translated *Don Quixote, Hamlet, El Little Prince* or *Alice's Adventuras in Wonderlandia* into Spanglish because he wants all voices to be heard and listened to, espe-cially the voices of the subalterns who have been silenced by the strong language.

4.2 A quest between originals: The *Popol Vuh*

For Stavans (2020b: 14) there is no primary and secondary text but rather a text and a previous text. In this way, he subverts many basic concepts of traditional translatology, such as those of the original or primary text and a translation or secondary text. "Originality is a tricky business" (Stavans 2018a: 28):

> En relación al concepto de "second original", esta opción, el Spanglish, actually prompts a third path: neither inglés nor español, crea una alter-nativa that we may want to call "tercer original". En mi propio caso, when I write a piece in casteñol —como lo hago ahora— it inhabits su propia estética and, para ser entendida en español o en inglés, it requires translation.
>
> (Stavans 2020a: 14–15)

In this context, the original "ought to be read as if written already in transla-tion – a translation without an original" (Stavans 2002: 88). This interplay between the original and second original is a recurring theme in litera-ture. Thus, José Saramago's *El hombre duplicado* [The Duplicated Man] describes the nightmare of not knowing who is the original and who is the copy. The *doppelgänger* is a recurrent theme that has fascinated writers such as Hoffmann, Dostoevsky, Maupassant, Henry James, Stevenson, Nerval, Poe, Wilde, Kafka, Wilde, Cortázar, and Queneau. It is the topic of *L'nomalie* by Hervé Le Tellier. This is also the idea behind Stavans' approach to self-translation, to which he has devoted a great deal of thought:

> he escrito cuentos en español que yo mismo have translated al inglés y que, when doing it, come out de forma distinta, con personajes diferentes y hasta endings that don't appear in the original. Confieso que a estas alturas I alone no sé cuál de las dos versiones es el original. In fact, prefiero un término utilizado originalmente por Singer: «second original». El autor que se auto-traduce se desdobla de tal manera que termina with two selves [...] El escritor que se auto-traduce exists en un permanente state of anxiety. En mi caso, I don't fully belong a la literatura mexicana o a la latinoamericana; en in the United States, I am seen también como una rara avis. Es decir, ni soy de aquí or from the other side. Este sentimiento, obviamente, isn't new; de hecho, en un siglo en el cual migration is the dividing line, esta ansiedad is rather ubiquituous, o al menos es una constante ascendente. To be dislocated, not to belong en ninguna parte, es ahora el sine qua non.
>
> (Stavans 2020a: 14)

For Stavans, both translation and self-translation are related to the idea of playing with mirrors, with duplicates. Books such as *On Self-Translation: Meditations on Language* (2018) and *I Love My Selfie* (2017) reflect on both these concepts. More specifically, in *I Love My Selfie*, there is a chapter on self-portraits from Rembrandt to Mapplethorpe and Ana Mendieta passing through Magritte and van Gogh. The art world is full of self-portraits, which are self-translations of the artist's mind, as in the case of Courbet and van Gogh, whose self-portraits have in turn been translated by pop art (Stavans 2017: 101), as though they were an infinite palimpsest or a Borgesian set of facing mirrors. According to Stavans, each and every one of Rembrandt's nearly 100 self-portraits is the same man yet a different one, since the self-translated self progressively changes over time and space. He regards Magritte's self-portraits as a rewriting of absence and anonymity though they are also "about exposure and celebration" (Stavans 2017: 102).

Similarly, Stavans understands self-translation as the self-portrait of a self-portrait, because his life is already a translation. He is a translated translator who lives in constant change and movement, travelling between languages and cultures. His work resembles the illusion created by Parmigianino in his self-portrait of his self-portrait (1524), in which he cleverly plays with a convex mirror's ability to offer a distorted representation of the person who looks into it, or in this case, his own image reflected in a mirror. Stavans is also like Vermeer, a painter who painted an artist as he was painting (*The Art of Painting*, 1966),

And beyond the infinite palimpsestic semantic play of Velázquez in *Las Meninas*, exquisitely portrayed by Foucault in *The Order of Things*, Stavans could also be situated in Velázquez's *Cristo en casa de Marta y María* [Christ in the House of Martha and Mary] (1618), where repetition, imitation, mirrors, and rewriting are the elements of a veritable theory of self-translation. Stavans would also have felt comfortable in *The Gallery of Archduke Leopold in Brussels* (1654–1670) by David Teniers the Younger, or in the 1747 self-portrait of Joshua Reynolds, in which the painted self gazes out at the spectator who is viewing the painting.

And he could also be observing the photographs of Rose Sélavy (1921) by Man Ray, which are in turn a self-translation of Marcel Duchamp (who also was subsequently rewritten in the work of Yasumasa Morimura). Stavans can be found in the image of the rear-view mirror in Alexander Rodchenko's photo entitled *Chauffeur* (1933) or in the self-photographs of Cindy Sherman, in which she uses her re-invented selves to critique the American way of life.

Stavans is fascinated by the stories of stories of stories. Perhaps that is why he recently decided to "translate" (and I write the verb in quotation marks) the *Popol Vuh*. This original translation is a very clear example of his quest between the original and his translations, between the second and the third original. The *Popol Vuh* is one of the few oral narratives that have survived the challenges of time and history. In fact, very few creation stories (about the origin and cosmology of the world and the forces of good and evil) from the indigenous cultures of the Americas, prior to the Spanish conquest, have reached us in written form.

The *Popol Vuh*, the sacred book of the Maya, is a story of resistance and defiance. It is thus a fascinating text for any translator. Although it was written shortly after the Spanish conquest by members of the K'iche' nobility in what is today Guatemala, the author is unknown. The original sixteenth-century text, written in the K'iche' language using the Latin alphabet, has been lost. Furthermore, this *Popol Vuh* is thought to be a copy that the author or authors transcribed from an original they possessed or were forced to recall from memory because the Spanish destroyed thousands of codices.

The oldest surviving copy of the *Popol Vuh* is a transcription of the K'iche' text by the Dominican friar, Francisco Ximénez, in 1701. He is also the author of the first known translation into Spanish. Unlike other Spaniards, he showed his admiration for indigenous cultures by learning various indigenous languages. Father Ximénez transcribed the manuscript from K'iche' into K'iche' and then translated it from K'iche' into Spanish.

This is the copy of the *Popol Vuh* that has been handed down to us since the K'iche' manuscript written in the Latin alphabet in the sixteenth century has been lost. One can only guess the extent to which the Western Christian perspective of Father Ximénez might have influenced his translation. The French *abbé*, Charles Etienne Brasseur de Bourbourg, first published the complete work in 1861. Since then, there have been numerous editions and translations.

The *Popol Vuh* is the great book of the K'iche' culture. It begins with the origin of everything, and is a story of tribal power and conflict, the emergence of the Mayan nation, the world above and the world below. The main characters are known as the Hero Twins, portrayed as dual complementary forces in order to better fight against the forces of evil. The book is also fascinating because it contains elements that seem to predict magical realism and others that refer to cross-breeding, as also occurs in "Kafka and His Precursors".

It is hardly surprising that the *Popol Vuh* fascinated Stavans. It is a text from a pre-Columbian codex written in Mayan hieroglyphs, which was lost. The 'original' text is the fruit of oral tradition and was the work of an anonymous author in K'iche', one of the Mayan languages, using the Latin alphabet. Furthermore, this is a text, whose first 'author' was a collector of oral histories. As such, he is the 'author' who rewrote an oral text, which has been handed down to us in a version that was translated by a Christian rewriter. Stavans emphasizes this in his essay at the end of his *Popol Vuh*, which he significantly titles "Retelling the Tale":

> As with the Bible, *Gilgamesh*, the *Iliad* and *Odyssey*, and other ancient books, the shaping of this collection of sacred K'iche' tales started through oral tradition. It was written down after the Spanish conquest, sometime in the middle of the sixteenth century, in part as a rescue effort after the devastation the indigenous community had experienced at the hands of the Europeans. The travel from the spoken to the printed word is, needless to say, treacherous. So much was lost in the process.
>
> (Stavans 2020e: 172)

Such a palimpsest could not leave any translator indifferent, especially a palimpsestic translator, whose translations strive to give a voice to all those who no longer have one. Stavans' translation (2020e) of the *Popol Vuh* is significantly subtitled "A Retelling". His translation does not attempt to transport the reader back into the past but rather strives to bring the text into the present. Consequently, even though his translation is faithful to the basic content of the text, it recreates and expands the original. In this sense, it is similar to other adaptations, recreations, and translations of the *Popol Vuh* in different languages (including the theatrical and musical adaptations), which acquaint the contemporary reader with a pivotal book on indigenous identity that has been silenced for centuries.

This retelling (or Stavans' original) is accompanied by the superb illustrations of Gabriela Larios. Indeed, there are various multimodal translations of the *Popol Vuh*, which take the form of musical adaptations, children's literature, theatrical productions, and even a symphonic poem. In this way, each medium and each new author add meaning to a text that began its life as a translation. Today, the text is a secondary original, an original translation:

> Interestingly, given the dozens of translations, adaptations, and appropriations the *Popol Vuh* has fostered since then, its refashioning is as alive today as it was before it became a physical book. Like speakers, translators are never innocent. Objective as they purport to be, they invariably add and take away based on an overt or unconscious agenda.
>
> (Stavans 2020e: 172)

Stavans himself says that his 'translation' of the *Popol Vuh* is really 'a recalibration', a new twist, a fresher way of telling stories that have already been told. During a stay in Oxford, he stumbled upon a copy of Charles and Mary Lamb's *Tales from Shakespeare* (1907):

> I always loved what the Lamb siblings did with the Bard, but I had forgotten about it. This time around, reading their charming adaptations of Shakespeare's plays generated in me an urge to embark on a similar project about a pre-Hispanic classic. Soon after, I also read Peter Ackroyd's version of *The Canterbury Tales* (2009), Arshia Sattar's adaptation of *The Ramayana* (2016), as well as Neil Gaiman's *Norse Mythology* (2017), a reimagining. Yes, that's exactly what I was after: an old text with a new voice; that is, not a translation per se but a recalibration.
>
> (Stavans 2020e: 173)

Stavans creates and recreates his translation, his second or third original, thanks to the fact that hundreds of years ago Francisco Ximénez did the same. This centuries-old translation, however, has been the object of criticism: "Some portray Father Ximénez's effort as an appropriation. He first did a translation in two columns, with K'iche' on the left and Spanish on the right, and then he produced a prose version" (Stavans 2020e: 174).

Stavans analyzed these texts along with others in Spanish, French, and German before making his own translation. He was, of course, aware that none of them, not even his, could be neutral. Like other scholars, he thus acknowledged that Father Ximénez's translation, like his own and like all other translations, is inevitably biased. It could not be otherwise. Centuries ago, this first version of the *Popol Vuh* served as a guide for Christian doctrine, and inevitably suffered from certain gaps in Father Ximénez's knowledge of the K'iche' language and culture:

> Father Ximénez was certainly an unreliable translator. He shaped parts in a way that allowed the text to be used as a conduit for the Christian doctrine. Subsequent scholars, doing comparative work on his versions of *Popol Vuh*, have described his knowledge of K'iche' language and culture as limited, even biased.
>
> (Stavans 2020e: 174)

Stavans had all of this in mind when he translated the *Popol Vuh*. Nevertheless, he observes the following:

> to me his effort, misguided as it might have been, is an act of courage that validates the quest of the K'iche' people. How much of the story is his? In what sense is the enabler responsible for what is ultimately being enabled? Was Father Ximénez also a "reteller"? So many other hands — amanuenses, interpreters, and so on — are at work here, pushing the reader to question what is authentic and what is invention.
>
> (Stavans 2020e: 175)

Moreover, in these successive layers of originals and rewritings of a book from the distant past, which is about the mythical origin of the world and the universe, Stavans also acknowledges the influence of the *Popol Vuh* by Ermilo Abreu Gómez as well as of many other versions (Stavans 2020e: 175–176). With this translation of a historical text, Stavans wants to acquaint a non-academic audience with the *Popol Vuh* by bringing the text from the past into the present, rather than by transporting the contemporary reader back into the past. There is a translation by Bartolomé de las Casas that does not include any English words that were not in use after 1552. At the other extreme is Edith Grossman, who uses words like *cool* or *awesome* in her translation of *Don Quixote*. Stavans' chooses the middle road and does not use either modern slang or words from the time of Father Ximénez. When he cannot find a suitable equivalent, he uses the K'iche' term and then expands it in English.

The objective of his retelling is to make a text of the distant past accessible to contemporary readers. He regards the *Popol Vuh* as a key book about origin and creation, which is as relevant as *The Books of Chilam Balam, Beowulf,* the *Odyssey,* and the *Northern Sagas.* On a more personal level, it was also an important book during his childhood in Mexico in the early 1970s. He is mainly interested in showing rather than telling. At the same time, the *Popol Vuh* is full of the echoes of other books, such as the *Old Testament.* These dialogues with other texts transform the original into a hybrid, as was, for example, the *Iliad.* Since it is a retelling, Stavans' original is a return to the oral tradition. It is not a straightforward translation, although it respects and pays tribute to the original. By respecting the original text, Stavans 're-dresses' the text for a twenty-first-century reader.

The *Popol Vuh* tells a retelling just as Father Ximénez retold a retelling, which helped to perpetuate this text. And so does Stavans. Both accomplish this through translation. Indeed, Stavans retells the retelling of a retelling. The *Popol Vuh* is a book about survival, which was created by a certain collectivity. It is about survival over time but it is also about hierarchies and power. In fact, the *Popol Vuh* is about dualisms though the Hero Twins are not exclusive but complementary, and the underworld is more interesting than the upperworld. As Stavans says, quoting Umberto Eco, it is not what it says but what it means

In Chen Yang's Chinese translation (for the Hunan Literature and Art Publishing House in 2022) of Stavans' 'translation' of the *Popol Vuh,* Stavans reflects on what it means to translate. He acknowledges that to translate is to embark on a journey and travel between spaces and languages to transform and clothe the text in new attire. In this new Chinese origin of this book on origin, which is of uncertain origin, Stavans states that translation leaves no one untouched:

> I am attracted to books with questionable origins whose ultimate form was shaped by translation. The *Popol Vuh* is a prime example. It wasn't "written" at a specific time and place. Its birth was in the form of oral tradition in K'iche', a language that, like all languages, changed every time the story was told. That is, the narrative didn't have a single author but a collectivity, which made its content mutate over centuries. Then, around the Spanish conquest, it was written down, a transcription that entails a form of translation.

For Stavans, the translation completes the original. Translation adds meaning but never subtracts it. It is the same text, yet it is not. The translator is an interpreter, a reader, and never an innocent creator that always reads a text in the same way.

> That transcription had a tangible beginning, middle, and end. It in turn became translated into other languages. The result builds a structure of

concentric circles: each time a new language is added, the *Popol Vuh* gains an audience. Is it the same book that the K'iche' hold in their heart? Yes and no. Translators are interpreters: they allow the book to travel *through their own views*. There is no such a thing as an innocent translation. Of course, some translators are more "loyal" than others. As it is impossible, according to Heraclitus, to read the same book twice (by definition, the reader's changes), each translation is biased. All translators are commentators.

Stavans' preface to the Chinese translation of his *Popol Vuh* leaves little doubt that he is the paradigmatic example of a Borgesian translator.

4.3 A Borgesian translator

Jorge Luis Borges mentions translation in various of his short stories, such as "Two Ways to Translate" (1926), "The Homeric Versions" (1932), "The Translators of *The 1001 Nights*" (1935), "An Examination of the Work of Herbert Quain" (1941), "On William Beckford's *Vathek*" (1951), "The Enigma of Edward Fitzgerald" (1951), "Averroes's Search", "The Circular Ruins" (1940), "The Gospel according to Saint Mark", "Borges and I", "The Doer", *The Universal History of Infamy* (1935), *Fictions* (1944), and *El Aleph* (1949).

In all these writings and many more, Borges argues that a translation is not inferior to the original and suggests that the concept of the 'definitive text' is a fallacy. So-called 'originals' are as much 'drafts' as translations are. The translator is the best reader of a text, which is why his interpretation invariably enriches it. With each new translation, new readings are incorporated, depending on the social environment and historical moment. Do translations age, or is it the texts that precede them? In any case, that is why no translation is definitive.

Thus, for example, in his *Universal History of Infamy*, Borges reworks selected pre-texts through linguistic and cultural appropriations. He displaces those pre-texts to the fringes in order to create unexpected meanings in a new context (Waisman 2005: 12). This confirms that Borges conceives translation as a process of creation, similarly to Octavio Paz in his 1971 essay "Translation: Literature and Literality", where he asserts that poetic translation is an act of creation, never of mimesis. In "The Homeric Versions", Borges also states that translation has a mobile and changing nature, which gives different perspectives on a mutable fact. The concept of the 'definitive text' corresponds, he says, only to exhaustion.

Borges champions translations that are different, according to the translator. For example, regarding the translations of *The Thousand and One*

Nights, he says that there are many books with that title. And once again Stavans follows Borges because both elect to be that creative translator who, as Borges assures us, cuts, expands, manipulates, and falsifies the original. That is why he (and doubtlessly Stavans as well) is most impressed by the translations that are the least equivalent. For that reason, in "Aladdin and the Wonderful Lamp", it does not matter that the original has never been found because, according to Borges, the translator has as much right to add stories as the original storytellers:

> The most famous tale of *The Thousand and One Nights* is not found in the original version. It is the story of Aladdin and the magic lamp. It appears in Galland's version, and Burton searched in vain for an Arabic or Persian text. Some have suspected that Galland forged the tale. I think the word forged is unjust and malign. Galland had as much right to invent a story as did those *confabulatores nocturni*. Why shouldn't we suppose that after having translated so many tales, he wanted to invent one himself, and did?
>
> (Borges 1980/1984: 573)

With all these reflections in mind, Stavans creates his translations. He doubtlessly recalls "The Homeric Versions", in which Borges affirms that in the translation of the classics "the first time is already the second time" because we are previously acquainted with them. The implication is that intralinguistic interpretations are also translations.

Within this conception of translation, the game of mirrors involving both authors and translators is evocative of the manuscript that Cervantes purchased in the Toledo market and which had to be translated. It also reminds us of the many authors of interest to Borges because of his fixation with the concept of authorship: Carlyle, who pretended that the *Sartor Resartus* was the partial version of another work published in Germany by another author; the Castilian rabbi, Moisés de León, who disseminated one of his own writings as the work of a Palestinian rabbi of the third century; Shakespeare, whose *Hamlet* includes a scene in which a tragedy is represented that is more or less that of *Hamlet*; or, finally, the strange game of ambiguities in the second part of *Don Quixote*, in which the protagonists have read the first part of the novel.

At the end of the "Partial Magic in the Quixote", Borges asks himself about this obsession with repetition, which centuries later still persists and is very much alive. He also wonders why we are so afraid of the recurring game of duplicates and false origins. He asks why we are concerned that there is a map included in a map and that the thousand and one nights are inside the volume of *The Thousand and One Nights*. Why are we uneasy that Don Quixote is a reader of *Don Quixote*, and Hamlet, a spectator of *Hamlet*? Borges answers that he believes that this disquiet arises because such inversions suggest that if fictional characters can be readers or spectators, we, as readers or spectators, can be fictitious (Borges 1952/1989: 47). Could this be what Ilan Stavans also suggests?

He evidently agrees with Borges when he affirms, "No soy de aquellos que místicamente prejuzgan que toda traducción es inferior al original. Muchas veces he comprobado, o he podido sospechar, lo contrario"[1] (Waisman 2005: 183). According to Borges, an original is often unfaithful to its translation. That is why he states at the beginning of "Two Ways to Translate" that he dislikes the old adage, *traduttore traditore traditore*. Original and translation are concepts that are diluted with fuzzy boundaries, as in "The Enigma of Edward Fitzgerald" (*Other Inquisitions*), where the protagonist finds his destiny as a writer in a foreign text.

It is this way of understanding the translation and original, the text and the previous text, that Stavans adopts. Stavans lives in Uqbar, a place he discovered with Borges, which arises from the conjunction of a mirror and books. Like Borges' Library of Babel, Stavans' universe is composed of an indefinite and perhaps infinite number of galleries, where, like Borges, he dreams that the burnished surfaces hold and promise infinity.

Stavans gives a practical demonstration of the dissolution of binary oppositions: "My aim is to convey not my nationality but my *transnationality*. To succeed, the original ought to be read as if written already *in* translation – a translation without an original" (Stavans 2002: 88). For this reason and perhaps inspired by Isaac Singer (Stavans 2021c: 97), he speaks of himself not as an original but as a second original (Stavans 2020a: 14), just like Borges' delightful story "Borges and I" in *The Doer* (1960):

> The other one, the one called Borges, is the one things happen to. I walk through the streets of Buenos Aires and stop for a moment, perhaps mechanically now, to look at the arch of an entrance hall and the grillwork on the gate; I know of Borges from the mail and see his name on a list of professors or in a biographical dictionary. I like hourglasses, maps, eighteenth-century typography, the taste of coffee and the prose of Stevenson; he shares these preferences, but in a vain way that turns them into the attributes of an actor. It would be an exaggeration to say that ours is a hostile relationship; I live, let myself go on living, so that Borges may contrive his literature, and this literature justifies me. It is no effort for me to confess that he has achieved some valid pages, but those pages cannot save me, perhaps because what is good belongs to no one, not even to him, but rather to the language and to tradition. Besides, I am destined to perish, definitively, and only some instant of myself can survive in him. Little by little, I am giving over everything to him, though I am quite aware of his perverse custom of falsifying

and magnifying things. Spinoza knew that all things long to persist in their being; the stone eternally wants to be a stone and the tiger a tiger. I shall remain in Borges, not in myself (if it is true that I am someone), but I recognize myself less in his books than in many others or in the laborious strumming of a guitar. Years ago I tried to free myself from him and went from the mythologies of the suburbs to the games with time and infinity, but those games belong to Borges now and I shall have to imagine other things. Thus my life is a flight and I lose everything and everything belongs to oblivion, or to him. I do not know which of us has written this page.

(Borges 1960/1964: 246)

I do not know which of us is writing this page. Borges repeatedly speaks of repetition. He reminds us that works like *The Thousand and One Nights* or *Don Quixote* do not have a single origin but stem from authors and translators who find manuscripts and translate them. This is also the case of Borges' *Homeric Versions*, where the first time is already the second. In my opinion, Stavans' translations are the exemplification of Borges' theories. For example, the dedication of his *Little Príncipe* reads as follows:

Pido apologies a los children por dedicarle este book a un grown-up. Pero tengo una Good excusa: este grown-up es el best amigo I have ever tenido. Yo tengo otra excusa también: este grown-up entiende everythin, hasta books pa' children. Y tengo una third excuse: este grown-up vive en rancia, where él tiene hambre y frío y necesita to be comforted. Yo quiero dedicar este book al niño que este grown-up once fue. Todos los grown-ups fueron once niños (pero lo mayoría lo ha olvidado). So voy a alterar mi dedicación:
A Léon Werth, el little niño que was (Stavans 2016: 7)

In this fragment we find strategies that are consistently applied throughout the translation, or rather throughout the second (or third?) original. Apart from the obvious mixture of languages that gives way to Spanglish, there are other interesting features such as the use of *yo* [I] in places where it is unnecessary. The syntax of both Spanish and English is interwoven to violate rules in peninsular Spanish such as the non-use of the upside-down exclamation mark at the beginning of an interjection or the upside-down question mark at the beginning of a question. Though very subtle, these are clear signs of Stavans' opposition to the norms of the *Real Academia Española*.

Also revealing is the use of *pa*, which reflects the de-hierarchization so typical of Stavans, who deconstructs the dividing line between high culture and popular culture. Other examples include *dedicatión* as well as others such as *landié, laugheó,* and *consolatión,* where the accent mark is evidence of the creativity of the translator when it comes to interweaving cultures. There are also other constructions such as the gerund *wandereando*:

> I'm fascinated by the act (and art) of retranslation. What books have merited more than one rendition? How does each translator change the original? To what extent is a translation defined by the time and place in which it is made? [...] I also believe the original can be disloyal to the translation.
>
> (Stavans in Kellman 2013: 4, 10)

Perhaps because it is a classic that addresses issues of human relations in general, *Le Petit Prince* is open to many interpretations. Stavans' translation is certainly much more than a mere linguistic transfer, in that it gives voice to a way of speaking of an entire community. As I was reading it, it reminded me (despite the evident differences) of the version of Juan Porras, *Er Principito* (2017), who translated Saint-Exupéry's work into Andalusian. Porras' intention was to revindicate a variety of peninsular Spanish whose speakers are the object of disdain and even rejection by those who speak other varieties.

The predominance and at certain times in the history of Spain, the imposition of Castilian Spanish has caused Andalusian to be associated with poverty-stricken areas, especially during certain time periods. Andalusian has also been regarded as a 'humorous' variety, good for telling jokes. However, it also has more pejorative connotations as reflected in series and movies, in which characters with a low cultural level are often dubbed in Andalusian. This also occurs in literature (as is the case of the waiter in the small Barcelona cafe in *The Shadow of the Wind* by Carlos Ruiz Zafón, which is so difficult to translate). This is the context of Juan Porras's translation, which has received a great deal of criticism (Marín 2019: 89–92). In his excellent study, David Marín (2019: 79) understands this rewriting as a *traducción identitaria* [identitarian translation] that has opted for an alternative orthography that tries to graphically reproduce the vernacular pronunciation of the speakers of the Guadalhorce Valley in Málaga (ibid.: 80). Marín writes:

> Una beh, kuando yo tenía zeih z'añiyoh, bi un dibuho mahnífiko en un libro a tento'e la zerba bihen ke ze yamaba "*Histoires Vecues* (Ihtoria bibíah)". En é ze figuraba a una bixa boa tragándoze una fiera.
>
> (Porras Blanco 2017: 9)

And ends as follows:

> ¡Konke zè guenoh! No me báyaih dehà tan trihte: ehkribirme de zegía
> k'a guerto é …
>
> (Porrah Blanko 2017: 94)

The Andalusian translation of Huan Porrah Blanko not only transmits the
accent through the spelling, but also affects the lexicon and morphosyntax,
as explained by Marín (2019: 80–81):

> La separación de la norma estándar española no es únicamente ortográ-
> fica Algunas elecciones léxicas y morfosintácticas revelan igualmente
> la voluntad de utilizar esta variedad dialectal en todos los niveles
> lingüísticos, ya que uno de los objetivos de este tipo de traducciones es
> demostrar que las variedades no estándares poseen la misma capacidad
> comunicativa y la misma riqueza literaria que la variedad ejemplar ante
> la que se presentan como alternativa.[2]

Just as Stavans mixes lexical units belonging to different hierarchies, Porrah
foregrounds features that the academia usually relegates to the background:
the level of language used by the translator is much lower than that of the
original text. Juan Porras' vindication is not only in defence of Andalusian
but also in defence of the least prestigious varieties, those that are spoken
by the most marginalized social classes (Marín 2019: 87).

Despite the evident difference in context, both of these translations represent a political vindication, namely, translation as a form of resistance
against a dominant language (Marín 2019: 83). In the case of *Er Principito*,
the struggle is between Andalusian and Castilian Spanish. Stavans' fight
is against peninsular Spanish and English. In any case, both Marín and
Stavans agree that there is not one Andalusian but many, just as there is not
one Spanglish but a wide variety (as Stavans observes in the prologue of his
Alice's Adventuras in Wonderlandia).

Another parallelism is the fact that both translators reject the prescrip-
tions of the Spanish Royal Academy. This is not only reflected in their language use, but also in their evident desire to throw off the shackles of any
type of colonialist imposition. It is hardly a coincidence that both translations are published in Tintenfass, a publisher that focuses on minority
languages. This same publishing house is the one that has published *The
Little Prince*, translated into Bolognese, Franco-Provençal, Patois Vaudois,
Strasbourg Alsatian, Parmigian, Senegalese Creole, and Pashto, among
many others. In this context (and as mentioned in the previous chapter),
Stavans' English-Spanish preface to *El Little Prince* begins with some very

revealing statements regarding the disappearance of minority languages and the difficult birth of new ones (Stavans 2016: 3).

In the same spirit, Stavans 'translada' Carroll's *Alice in Wonderland* into Spanglish and published it in Evertype. This publisher has also published translations of the same work in Latin, Yiddish, Karacháyo-Balkaro, Neapolitan, Uropi, and others, not to mention a version for the dyslexic. As previously mentioned, Stavans' *Alice's Adventuras in Wonderlandia* is a second original whose foreword clearly states that this third (?) original wishes "adderar voces y no substraerlas" (Stavans 2021d: vi). This is in consonance with both the translingual literature and the postmonolingual era described in the first chapter.[3] For these reasons, Stavans' text aspires to be one more original that will help to complete the first text by Lewis Carroll:

> There are those who dirán que hay otras maneras de transladar Lewis Carroll al Spanglish. Estoy de acuerdo: si hay 22 translaciones de *Don Quixote* al English y 12 de *Crime and Punishment* de Dostoyevsky, por qué no aspirar once again a la pluralidad?[4]
>
> (Stavans 2021d: vi)

In this new original, Stavans also changes many cultural references:

> el carácter de Pat es Irish, pero yo lo he hecho Brazilian; he remplazado las referencias a William the Conqueror con otras a Colón, Isabel La Católica, Torquemada, la Santa Inquisición, el Ché Guevara, César Chávez y otros episodes of Hispanic historia; Shakespeare se hace Cervantes y el Cheshire Cat en el Gato de Cheshire; y he llamado a las tres hermanas Elese, Laicia y Tili[5]
>
> (Stavans 2021d: vi–vii)

The expressions are often associated with non-academic forms of speech (*pa'*) or the use of the exclamation and question mark only at the end of sentences, contrary to the norm of the Spanish Royal Academy.

> Either el pozeo era muy Deep, o ella cayó muy slowly, porque ella had plenty de tiempo as she went down pa'ver about her and pa' wonderear qué was going to pasar next [...] "Caramba!" pensó Alicia pa' sí misma, "after tanto fall as this, yo voy a pensar nothing de tumbling down las escaleras!"
>
> (Stavans 2021d: 9)

4.4 Stavans' other languages: *Don Quixote* in images

The translation of cultural references is a way of situating and relocating stories from the distant past in a more contemporary context. Stavans has previously used this type of rewriting to create second and third originals. However, he also uses images, a language that transcends words. This is the case of one of his *Don Quixotes*, which takes the form of a graphic novel and which he translated into English and Spanglish (2018, Penn State Press).

This linguistic and visual translation is a tribute to the work that, as Stavans himself confesses, has most influenced him. This original is Stavans' translation of 30 of the 125 chapters of *Don Quixote*. This translation is (un)faithful to another original that, as Cervantes explains, was actually a translation from the Arabic-Cide Hamete at his purest, "Borges and I", the Moorish translator, and the second Christian author. And during this process of original, secondary authors, translated but unknown, it is impossible to forget Avellaneda, the impostor of Cervantes' *Don Quixote*, whom Stavans also mentions in the second part of his graphic novel, where he reflects on the concept of authorship and the implications of creativity and originality.

This graphic novel, metafictional in places, sometimes transports us to modern times. For example, there are feminist banners that read "Women of the World Unite" in a world of drones, laptops, cabs, and airplanes. We find Antonio de Nebrija, Erasmus of Rotterdam, Antoni Gaudí and the *Sagrada Familia*, *America* by Franz Kafka, *Lolita* by Vladimir Nabokov, *One Hundred Years of Solitude* by Gabriel García Márquez, *Beloved* by Toni Morrison, *The Catcher in the Rye* by J. D. Salinger, and, of course, Jorge Luis Borges and his "Pierre Menard". There are also characters from *Star Wars* and *Sesame Street*, and the inn where Don Quixote stays is the "Flamingo Motel". This is all feasible because for Stavans, *Don Quixote* is an ageless book with infinite space for all generations. It is a dialogue with the past and the future.

This original translation, this second original that Stavans translates with both words and images, also speaks of translation, which he defines as "one of the most arduous endeavors in the entire world". This *Don Quixote*, rewritten as a graphic novel, does not have Cervantes, Cide Hamete, Avellaneda, or Stavans as its only authors. It is also the work of Roberto Weil, the illustrator. His images make us wonder about ourselves and the world around us. In our visual culture, graphic novels and comics are a way of reaching the many people who are more attracted to images than to words. In fact, these genres sometimes address deeply controversial issues. Images that read the world are a way of being in our visual society, characterized by an iconic twist:

> the emergence of the Internet as a digital and visual storage medium and the overproduction of pictures and images in our media society

– all hint at an iconic turn […] Yet talk of an iconic turn is not just a reference to the increasing importance of visual phenomena of everyday culture. This turn has led to a new epistemological awareness of images in the study of culture. Linked to a critique of knowledge and language, it seeks to promote a visual literacy that has been poorly developed in Western societies since Plato's hostility toward images and logocentrist trends in philosophy. The dominance of language in Western cultures has long marginalized the study of visual cultures.

(Bachmann-Medick 2016: 245)

The images, which are more meaningful than words, drive the plot. It is thus hardly surprising that in this graphic novel, the (Borgesian) mirrors are an important point of reflection:

Mirrors invite us to meditate on who we are. Or who we aren't, since everything depends on perception. On which side of the mirror do we live? Is the knight I'm looking at asking the same question I am asking right now?

– wonders Don Quixote as he gazes into the mirror at the end of the first part of the novel. These reflections of Stavans' Quixote remind us that in the second of his "Seven Nights" (1980), Borges confesses that his two nightmares are labyrinths and mirrors. Both are closely related, because, as he observes, two facing mirrors are sufficient to construct a labyrinth. Moreover, on that second night, Borges assures us that another of his recurring dreams is masks. These are also the dreams (or nightmares) of Ilan Stavans.

One may agree or disagree with the idea of mirrors, infinite books, and stories that contemporary authors write within or from other stories. Nonetheless, it cannot be denied that these second and third originals have a long tradition in the arts. Examples include the *Don Quixote* of Honoré Daumier, Gustave Doré, Pablo Picasso, Salvador Dalí, or André Masson, but also the opera by Jules Massenet as well as the ballet by Marius Petipa and Luwig Minkus, staged by the Bolshoi. There is the *Quichotte* of Salman Rushdie or that of Kathy Acker. These are also rewritings of a classic work. Rewritings have also appeared of other well-known stories, such as the feminist translations of traditional fairy tales, for example, the very different versions of *Little Red Riding Hood* by Angela Carter, Carmen Martín Gaite, or Niki Daly's *Pretty Salma*, the African version.

Stavans also uses the graphic novel genre in *Mr. Spic Goes to Washington* (2008, with illustrations by Roberto Weil) and *A Most Imperfect Union: A Contrarian History of the United States* (2014, with illustrations by Lalo

Alcaraz), which is an alternative account of the history of the United States, given by the voices of the voiceless. A few years earlier, we also find *Latino U.S.A. A Cartoon History* (2000, illustrated by Lalo Alcaraz), which is a chronicle of Latino culture with a comic twist, narrated by storytellers as contradictory as Cantinflas, Captain America, and Stavans himself.

In all these cases, Stavans intralinguistically rewrites the story not only in words but also in illustrations. In *El Iluminado* (2012), Steve Sheinkin, the illustrator, transforms Stavans into a comic book character (who also appears at the end of *Don Quixote*). *El Iluminado* is a self-translation that uses both words and images. In this graphic novel, English is mixed with certain Spanish phrases to translate into various languages and semiotic systems the real events that happened to Luis de Carvajal the Younger at the end of the sixteenth century. It describes the Spanish conquest, King Ferdinand and Queen Isabela, the Inquisition, Catholicism, and the persecution of the Jews.

In his translation of *Once@9:53 am. Terror en Buenos Aires*, Stavans once again uses images, though in this case, they are photographs. In this *fotonovela* co-authored with Marcelo Brodsky (Stavans and Brodsky 2016), photography is used by the main character (who also happens to be a photographer) to translate the terrorist attack against the AMIA (Asociación Mutual Israelita Argentina), the Jewish community centre in the Argentine capital, on July 18, 1994 at 9:53 am. This *fotonovela* was first published in Spanish in Buenos Aires by Asunto Impreso so that it would also reach a wider popular audience instead of only an academic one.

This *fotonovela* is an excellent example of how gazing is a way of narrating the world. The question is who the viewer actually is when individuals see themselves reflected in the eyes of others. And how does the individual, who is looking while being looked at, understand this divide? Or vice versa.

And indeed, our way of gazing at the other reveals a great deal about who we are. Furthermore, it reveals the images and words that we have chosen to narrate, paint, and translate reality. The images in *Eleven@9:53 am. Terror en Buenos Aires* translate a polycentric world of different gazes, of meanings that clash in the representation of different worlds. Like translations, images are forms of representation that produce and reproduce. Looking is translating the world in the language of images. Each image is a way of seeing, a way of writing. This is what John Berger did in *Ways of Seeing*, which consists of three image-only pictorial essays. In this book, Berger states that "seeing comes before words", that "seeing establishes our place in the surrounding world", and that "the relation between what we see and what we know is never settled" (Berger 1972). This *fotonovela* of Stavans is an example of Berger's words.

Regardless of whether we like these rewritings, these new translations are evidently a way of bringing the classics into the present through images and words. Stavans defines the classics as 'patient' books that survive trans-lations, which enrich them with new meanings:

> A literary classic is a book that knows how to be patient, a book with all the time on its hands, capable of waiting for the right readers to come by. It is also a book that "survives" translation. The classics are always in the process of being retranslated, in part because they are in the public domain but also because language ages, which prompts us to refashion them under a fresh new look [...] Translators are always pitching new versions as a way to supersede the inefficacies of their predecessors, only to produce, of course, equally ineffica-cious versions.
>
> (Stavans in Tang 2021: n.p.)

They are translations that are attuned to the way millions of people in our global society not just speak but live. Stavans states that translation is not an innocent act but rather a way to interpret and subvert. Translation, as Benjamin observed, revives and rejuvenates the original. Language is a mirror of social values, and in certain contexts such as this one, transla-tion is also an effective way of opposing the established norm by high-lighting the fact that monolingualism is fundamentally a political strategy. As the fox tells the Little Prince, that la language puede ser una source of misentendimiento.

With his second and third originals, Stavans forces us to reflect on contemporary borders represented by "border languages today: franglais, portunhol, hibriya, etc." (Stavans 2021d: viii) as well as other "middle-step" languages such as Yinglish that arose from migrations. Stavans' translations create a second text that reflects, as Borges said of *The Thousand and One Nights*, that the first text can give rise to many others, which enrich and complete the first original. This occurs because the translator, who is the best reader of the first text, extracts meanings that are in consonance with the target culture. Like Carroll, Stavans is against the univocity of language and, as Alice suggests to the Cheshire Cat, he plays at being on the other side of the mirror. Rewriting is a way of travelling to the other side of the looking glass. It is a way of *wandereando* in the garden of living flowers, knowing, like Tarari and Tarara, that we are someone else's dream.

As the Queen of Hearts warns Alice, a good memory (like the memory of a good translator) is a memory that works in both directions, backwards and forwards. As Borges (and later Stavans) points out, the translator has every right to add stories. The repetition that Pierre Menard wished to achieve is impossible, and furthermore, it is useless since, according to Borges, the first time is already the second time. Stavans' translations are not only located on the other side of the looking glass, but also in Tlön, where metaphysicians seek astonishment and where plagiarism does not exist, where things are duplicated and are only erased when we forget them.

Notes

1 I am not one of those people that mystically prejudges every translation to be inferior to the original. Many times I have verified, or I have suspected, precisely the opposite.
2 The difference from standard Spanish is not only orthographic. Certain lexical and morphosyntactic choices also reveal the desire to use this dialectal variety at all linguistic levels, since one of the objectives of this type of translation is to demonstrate that nonstandard varieties have the same communicative capacity and the same literary richness as the standard variety to which they are presented as an alternative [our translation].
3 It is worth highlighting that in this essay, Rushdie refers to Alice as someone who dares to cross a frontier: "To cross a frontier is to be transformed. Alice at the gates of Wonderland, the key to that miniature world in her grasp, cannot pass through the tiny door beyond which she can glimpse marvelous things until she has altered herself to fit into her new world. But the successful frontierswoman is also, inevitably, in the business of surpassing. She changes the rules of her newfound land: Alice in Wonderland, shape-shifting Alice, terrifies the locals by growing too big to be housed. She argues with Mad Hatters and talks back to Caterpillars and, in the end, loses her fear of an execution-hungry Queen when she, so to speak, grows up. You're nothing but a house of cards—Alice the migrant at last sees through the charade of power, is no longer impressed, calls Wonderland's bluff, and by unmaking it finds herself again. She wakes up" (Rushdie 2003: 415).
4 There are those who will say that there are other ways of translating Lewis Carroll into Spanglish. I agree: if there are 22 translations of *Don Quixote* into English and 12 of Dostoyevsky's *Crime and Punishment*, why not aspire once again to plurality [our translation]?
5 Pat is Irish, but I have made him Brazilian; I have replaced the references to William the Conqueror with others to Columbus, Isabel La Católica, Torquemada, the Inquisition, Ché Guevara, César Chávez and other episodes of Hispanic history; Shakespeare becomes Cervantes and the Cheshire Cat becomes the Gato de Cheshire; and I have called the three sisters Elese, Laicia and Tili [our translation].

5 In lieu of conclusion

In his preface to *Selected Translations, 2000–2020*, Stavans summarizes what translation means to him. Translating is a constant migration, a journey between identities; it is continuous movement between spaces, languages, and cultures. His texts are palimpsests, the sound of steps on a street that echo in other streets, much like the poem by Octavio Paz (1999) that is the epigraph of Stavans' volume of essays on Latino authors written by other Latino authors. He thus describes it as "a book about neighbors: not about who our neighbors are but about who we imagine them to be. Consequently, it is also about borders – or better, about crossing verbal and geographical borders" (Stavans 1999: 1).

This is a brilliant definition of translating. Translation is crossing borders and moving closer to those who, even without realizing it, are our neighbours. In this introduction, Stavans further manifests his obsession with borders and describes the United States as a society of migrants, whereas Latin America is "an archipelago of sovereign solitudes" (Stavans 1999: 2). This results in a transcultural and translingual library (Stavans 1999: 10).

Ilan Stavans is a scholar who leaves no one indifferent. As pointed out by Steven Kellman (2019), he has both enthusiastic admirers and harsh critics. Still, no one can deny that Stavans is in the vanguard of one of the most exciting schools of thought in contemporary translation. This new movement envisages the hybrid world of today, a world of millions of displaced people, as a world in constant translation. Perhaps it is Stavans' eagerness to democratize culture that causes him to transform Sor Juana Inés de la Cruz into a pop icon (Stavans 2018c) through reproductions of silkscreen prints, installations, and modern pictorial representations. For the same reason, he retells *Don Quixote* as a graphic novel.

In this same line, his publishing house, Restless Books, is deeply committed to the translation of the classics and their dissemination. More specifically, the Restless Books Classics re-envisions literary classics for contemporary audiences, whereas Classics Behind Bars brings classics

DOI: 10.4324/9781003323730-6

closer to incarcerated individuals. In 2016, Stavans created the Restless Books Prize for New Immigrant Writing to highlight works of fiction and nonfiction by first-generation migrants. The same publishing house also organizes a series titled Immigrant Writing Workshops. In the following description of these workshops, Stavans links migration with translation:

> These workshops not only inform Restless Books' mission but define it. Immigrants understand what it feels like to live in the margins, peripherally. My impression is that the syncopated dance between the center and the periphery is no longer what it used to be. The center today exists in a state of never-ending doubt, complicit in ancestral crimes that range from colonialism to appropriation. It is minorities who now set the tone of cultural change. They function as translators […] Translation is not just about languages; it is about the "coming across" among cultures. How does one navigate the marriage of sensibilities between authors and translators? How do you consider gender, ethnicity, and other identities to foster a more balanced and diverse relationship among all the people who are bringing cross-cultural works to the world?
>
> (Stavans in Tang 2021: n.p.)

This is even more relevant because, according to Stavans (which recalls the words of Edward Said and Salman Rushdie cited in the first chapter), "the theme of the twenty-first century is immigration" (Stavans in Tang 2021: n.p.). And it is translation that brings us closer to what is different:

> Translators open the window to the past to welcome fresh air. They are surveyors of what is significant somewhere else and want to bring that significance home. As we make room for new voices from the world, we must diversify the database of translators. If and when they come from a diverse background, what they propose is likely to be more heterogeneous. A theater teacher of mine used to say to me that what's important is not to give the audience what the audience wants but to teach the audience to want something else. A diverse army of translators will be able to achieve such an objective. The same goes for editors and, of course, publishers: we need otherness to be less alien.
>
> (Stavans in Tang 2021: n.p.)

In this respect, Stavans agrees with Viet Thanh Nguyen, the Vietnamese-American writer, who won the Pulitzer Prize in 2016 for his novel, *The Sympathizer*. In his superb anthology on refugee literature, Nguyen argues that we need stories that give a voice to the voiceless because listening to those voices is the first step, though certainly not the only one, to bringing about change:

> We need stories to give voice to a writer's vision, but also, possibly, to speak for the voiceless. This yearning to hear the voiceless is a powerful rhetoric but also potentially a dangerous one if it prevents us from doing more than listening to a story or reading a book. Just because we have listened to that story or read that book does not mean that anything has changed for the voiceless. Readers and writers should not deceive themselves that literature changes the world. Literature changes the world of readers and writers, but literature does not change the world until people get out of their chairs, go out in the world, and do something to transform the conditions of which the literature speaks. Otherwise literature will just be a fetish for readers and writers, allowing them to think that they are hearing the voiceless when they are really only hearing the writer's individual voice [...] That is a writer's dream, that if only we can hear these people that no one else wants to hear, then perhaps we can make you hear them, too.
>
> (Nguyen 2018: 12, 14)

The rewritings of Stavans continually remind us that we speak with borrowed words. They alert us to the fact that "translation studies today has left behind narrow Eurocentric definitions of translation as a univocal and unidirectional transfer of meaning from the source language to the target language, both of which are viewed as already polyvocal and hybrid" (Karpinski 2012: 4). In these translations

> neither the "original" nor the "author" can serve as a guarantor of meaning or truth because "texts" and "subjects" are not originary and unified, but always already derivative and heterogeneous, themselves constructed at the intersections of multiple languages and codes [...] translation is transformative rather than imitative in that it makes the target language "grow" at the same time as it ensures survival of the original by making a foreign text perform new meanings in the target culture.
>
> (Karpinski 2012: 7, 8)

For Stavans, translating is not knowing what our mother tongue is. It is feeling at home in a deterritorialized territory that never witnessed our birth, and where we dwell in a borderland between languages. Languages are considerably more than a collection of words because each word contains the DNA of an entire civilization. For that reason, a language is a way of envisioning the world. Languages and their words are always borrowed. These words do not really belong to us since they are palimpsests indelibly marked by the scars of previous meanings, redolent of those places that they used to inhabit, imbued with those scents and flavours that remind us that it is our responsibility not only to safeguard words but also to push them to the limit. Languages and words are living beings that reflect the world, the worlds where they are, where they were, and where they will be.

For Stavans, translating means knowing how to identify and express what words do not explicitly say. It signifies being able to narrate those stories, and to convey their myriad connotations, which are present in too vast a number to measure or count. It means knowing how to penetrate both the individual and collective mappings of associations which are the only true maps of meaning. Perhaps, as Borges observes in his essay "On Blindness" in *Seven Nights*, translating means letting go of the visible world in order to discover another.

Perhaps that is why Stavans is so fascinated by (self-)translators such as Samuel Beckett, who edited an anthology of Mexican poets without knowing Spanish. He is also captivated by many other contemporary translators and theorists whose approach to the act of translating bears little or no relation to mere interlinguistic transfer but rather to the celebration of Babel. Accordingly, in the preface to this book, Kellman writes that Stavans translates (mostly poetry) from languages that he knows, but also from others he does not know well or even at all. Stavans himself confesses this, while pointing out that he is not the only adherent to this tradition:

> I translate not only from languages I know—if it is at all possible to say that one knows a language—but from those I don't know. My heroes are John Florio, who made Montaigne feel comfortable in English and, on the way, defined Shakespeare; Richard Burton, whose *One Thousand and One Nights* is exquisite; Samuel Beckett, who rendered Sor Juana Inés de la Cruz and other colonial Mexican poets in Spanish without knowing a word of it; Joseph Brodsky, who wrote in English while anchored in Russian and vice versa; Jorge Luis Borges, who in 1943, in an essay on William Beckford's *Vathek*, argued that "the original is unfaithful to the translation"; and Adrienne Rich, who appreciated, perhaps disingenuously, that if language is power, silence is violence.
>
> (Stavans 2021a: xvi)

It is a feat of great daring and skill, a kind of Talmudic chutzpah, and at the same time, it also reflects an understanding of language and translation that Stavans shares with other translators. Perhaps some of the best known are Celia and Louis Zukofsky, who 'homophonically' translated the poetry of

Catullus by recreating the rhythms and music of the words. They thus managed to transform Latin verse into English diction at the expense of meaning and by giving priority to the signifier.

And, of course, there is Ezra Pound, whose translations reflect the energy of language, which he understood as a living being. When he translated, his goal was to transcend unitary meaning and to approach each word as though it were a sculpted image.

Pound's translations, the object of countless studies, have been both praised and reviled. He believed that it was necessary to translate *melopeia*, the music of words, when words are 'charged' with some musical property that further directs their meaning His second 'mark' of poetry was *phanopoeia*, the images evoked by words, which he conceived as a casting of images upon the visual imagination The third 'mark' was *logopoeia*, which is characteristic of poetry that uses words for more than just their direct meaning by stimulating the visual imagination and inducing emotional correlations.

According to Pound, author of the *Cantos*, no poetic translator can be faithful to the original: "Taint what a man sez [*sic*] but what he *means* that the traducer [*sic*] has got to bring over. The *implication* of the word" (Pound in Bassnett 2014: 151). In her analysis of Pound's translations, Bassnett highlights the word *traducer*, which Pound, quite ingeniously, chooses instead of *translator*.

> Traducer says a great deal about his response to the accusation of unfaithfulness to which he was himself periodically subjected. Pound was dismissive of the idea that a translator could faithfully reproduce an original, and all too aware of the kind of textual manipulations a good translator has to perform.
>
> (Bassnett 2014: 151)

Bassnett's last sentence reveals what it means to translate. It is also an accurate description of the way that many translators, including Stavans, work today. Her understanding of translation is in line with that of other contemporary scholars in Translation Studies, who are also translators. Examples include Susan Bassnett herself but also Gentzler, Johnston, Bellos, Bush, Arrojo, de Campo, Venuti, and Coldiron, to name but a few. All of them are translators and translation theorists who, despite certain differences, share the premise that "no text can be exactly reproduced in another language" (Bassnett 2014: 152) as well as the idea that translation as

> the betrayal of an original is nothing less than an absurd value judgement, based on an idealization of what is achievable by a translator

and on an outmoded hierarchical positioning of textual practice that relegates translation to a subsidiary marginal status.

(*id.*)

Today there is no doubt that translation and migration are phenomena that are closely linked (Polezzi 2012; Cronin 2006; Inghilleri 2017; Nergaard 2021; Woodsworth 2022), because migrating evidently implies changing territory, language, memory, and culture:

> Migration flows have introduced new cultural and linguistic diversity in previously more apparently homogeneous communities. The ways in which such movements and new settlements have changed the identity of their new locations, and have affected the feelings and practices of migrants and their new neighbours are particularly visible in local sites that are "in translation", belonging to no single, discrete language or cultural/ethnic group.
>
> (Wilson 2021: 148)

The spatial turn in Translation Studies has revealed that contemporary cosmopolitan spaces are a mishmash, a kaleidoscope. They are spaces in which one is continually travelling between languages and cultures, spaces whose inhabitants are always "drawn to, immersed in and preoccupied with translation, from its most narrow, literal sense as the interlingual transfer of meaning to its wider, figurative and metaphorical manifestations" (Woodsworth 2022: 1).

As we have seen, the literature of migrants is an "arena of discourse, the place where the struggle of languages can be acted out" (Rushdie 1992: 427). The literature of those who live in translation manages to bring us closer to a "a translational 'migrant' knowledge of the world" (Bhabha 1994: 306) in order to evaluate "uncertainty, displacement, the fragmented identity" (Hoffman 1999: 44). And, as Bhabha points out in "How Newness Enters the World", a title borrowed from *The Satanic Verses,* contemporary hybridization is "an empowering condition [...] insurgent and ironic" (Bhabha 1994: 324).

Translating, in all cases, but especially when it involves translating people who live in constant translation, is not merely an interlinguistic activity, but one with an infinitely wider scope:

> Instead of seeing translation merely as a movement of meaning across languages, cultures, and borders, we read translation as a relocating act: of meanings and texts but also of people and cultures. As a keyword of today's global culture, in fact, relocation commonly refers to the

redistribution of migrants, but it also describes the cultural and linguistic adjustments that people who move from one form of belonging to another know firsthand.

(Bertacco and Vallorani 2021: 1)

In "What Is Literature For?", Todorov (2007: 32) writes that he loves literature because it helps him to live even though it does not shield him from adverse experiences that can still wound him. Nonetheless, literature is so close to his heart because it is the medium that discovers worlds. It puts him in contact with other people, with other universes, and thus invites him to imagine other ways of conceiving and organizing that world. Literature thus reflects the social changes of each era; and our era is an era of hybridization and impurity, an era of infinite enrichment.

In this context, Stavans' literature and translations narrate the mixture (Onghena 2014) and bring this difference to light. However, they also reveal the gazes that construct this difference or those that construct it for us. They allow us to see who fashions this reality, who imposes it on us, and how it is categorized. It is all a question of looking and truly perceiving the other, always aware that any categorization is a construct and that the margin is a shared space, Consequently, cultures are never homogeneous, but are always impure, populated by differences, recycling, and palimpsests. And these factors are what enrich us all.

Hybrid translation and intermingled language bring us closer to what we do not know and to what makes us feel uneasy. It forces us to gaze into that in-between where everything is in motion, into that fissure between us and them, into that deterritorialized territory where there is multidimensional interconnection but no real structure. In this in-between, we are all hybrids, rewritings of others, Ariadne's threads, a mixture of stories that become much more than the sum of their parts.

The literature of migrants is transcultural in the sense of Fernando Ortiz's *Contrapunteo cubano del tabaco y el azúcar* (1940), which refers to transculturation as a process in which each part modifies the other. From this reciprocal transformation, a new reality emerges, independent of the previous one. The migrant culture and the culture of their interim homeland thus transform each other to create a hybrid literature. As García Canclini (1995) pointed out many years ago, hybridization is everything. It is the ongoing condition of human cultures. Hybridization is embedded in a network of concepts that also includes those of contradiction, difference, and inequality. Hybridity is intersection and transaction, and that is why it is "a translation term" (Canclini 1995: xliii).

In this context, Stavans invites us to scrutinize the asymmetries constructed by binary thinking. He encourages us to conclude that it is perhaps

possible to see otherness by unmasking its accomplices, who insist on rein-
forcing essentialisms. They emphasize the need for hierarchy and permanent immobility as opposed to change, movement, and interconnectedness.
In this context, being on the frontier is far from simple, because existing in
the neither here nor there between boundaries in the "Borderland" refers
to an intermediate state, to an in-between, which is very enriching but
which is also an open wound (Anzaldúa 1987: 25). Stavans' hybridization
provides an explanation for relational identities (in the sense of Édouard
Glissant). His processes of creolization invite us to understand difference
as enrichment.

This is Stavans' approach to translation, which states that "since there
can be no definitive reading, there can obviously be no definitive translation" (Bassnett 2015: 152). In the same way as in the Middle Ages (e.g.,
Chaucer) as well as in the sixteenth century, translation is not based on the
binary, hierarchical distinction between the original text and the translation
(see Bassnett in Bassnett and Bush 2006: 173). Translating is rather a dual
process that includes multiple and continuous rewritings that happen in the
present but must also consider the future of the new text, which will be an
original in its new context (Bush in Bassnett and Bush 2006: 25).

"Words are all we have", Samuel Beckett once remarked. Maybe
Stavans agrees. And perhaps this signifies that a translation always
involves going beyond. In other words, it means completing the original à
la Borges, opening a new path, and writing our melodies on other pentagrams. As Peter Stillman says in *City of Glass*, the translator must take all
the meanings of a word into consideration, even when those meanings are
contradictory. Words are not simply attached to things; they reveal their
essence.

The translator will listen to all the voices hiding within each word, and
thus embrace their silences, their uncertainties, the impurities of the borderline, and heteroglossic spaces of expressions such as *Wáchale*! The words
chosen by Stavans are those of the displaced, of those individuals who so
often have had to accept or admit to the atrocious without flinching. So,
when he translates poems from languages that he does not know, and when
he brings to light all the voices, silences, and insinuations within the words,
Stavans shows us that translating is not a mechanical task but rather a highly
creative one. This is translation as interpretation, or as the creation of a new
original:

> and hence as the rewriting *and* creation of a new "original" in another
> language. Recognizing the indeterminacy of literary texts on the one
> hand, and the impossibility of "faithful" translation on the other,
> liberates the translator from servitude to the source from which the

translation derives and undermines the old Romantic concept of authorship and at the same time revises simplistic notions of intentionality.

(Bassnett 2014: 153)

Stavans translates from Georgian, German, Russian, and Portuguese. Sometimes he does this by studying the language or the sounds. Other times he does it by reading texts by that author or by contemporary authors, or the translations of that author into other languages. Sometimes he translates through a third person, though the resulting translation is not only his alone but at the same time a translation of many. Isn't a text always a consequence of our previous readings, intertexts of intertexts? This is similar to Borges' references in "The Analytical Language of John Wilkins", where he places us on the other side, in the infinite combinations of letters and possible melodies.

When translating from languages he does not know, Stavans penetrates the interstices of words, listens to the signals that the words send him, and interprets the hints they give. He delves into their concatenations, and scrutinizes their past and future, but also their possible (dis)appearance. By regarding them as living beings, he is aware that he needs words to stay alive, and that words provide freedom from loneliness. As a result, the threads that interweave his senses create a vital fabric that makes all the stories interact.

Stavans' translations exemplify what so many contemporary translation theorists assert, namely, that translation is an interpretation (Coldiron 2016) and a rewriting that is always unfinished (Bassnett 2014). Translation is all the more exciting when it is less finite, and more of a *work* when there is less *text* (in Barthes' sense of the terms). Stavans' translations are vivid proof that the translator is also a writer (Bassnett and Bush 2006), and in that sense,

> that translation is not an act of preservations (of a definitive text), nor an act of recall (of a text that inevitably belongs to the past), but an act of transmission (of handing on a text in what is deemed an appropriate form) and of reimagination [...] Translation itself is constantly redrawing maps, redisposing the territories of language and cultures. Translation is *métissage*, interbreeding, hybridization, grafting, creolization [...] Translation does not merely register that change, that change's inevitability, but actively works to produce it.
>
> (Scott in Bassnett and Bush 2006: 109, 116)

In his translations, Stavans reimagines, (re)maps, reterritorializes, and changes in Scott's sense. He is constantly interweaving stories because he refuses to renounce any of the senses or feelings that permeate each word. In his case, the translator is a funambulist walking on a tightrope between different *topoi*. With each translation, as in the Aleph, he takes us into the past and into the future, creating things with words and words with things. As Stavans has shown us, translating can be much more than speaking with two voices. There are more voices and more hands that write in the hexagonal galleries through which the translator moves.

Like Borges, Stavans' translations seek the plural, and clearly transcend the old adage "traduttore, traditore". In the same way as the translators of the 1001 Nights, he searches for good apocrypha, knowing that there are only drafts, and that draft number nine is not inferior to the H. As in the *Universal History of Infamy*, the original is always unfaithful to the translation and each translation, which is a new reading, completes the original. Like Calvino's *If on a Winter's Night a Traveler*, the translator transmits the writable that is waiting to be written and the narratable that no one has ever told. To translate is to create, to recreate, and to move unceasingly between texts, languages, and cultures.

Bibliography

Adorno, Theodor. 1951/2005. *Minima Moralia*. New York: Verso.

Ahmad, Dohra, ed. 2019. *The Penguin Book of Migration Literature*. New York: Penguin.

Alvarez, Lizette. 1997. "It's the Talk of Nueva York: A Hybrid Called Spanglish", *The New York Times*. March 25, Section A, pp. 1, 30.

Anzaldúa, Gloria. 1987. *Borderlands/La Frontera: The New Mestiza*. San Francisco: Aunt Lute Books.

Akcan, Esra. 2012. *Architecture in Translation: Germany, Turkey and the Modern House*. Durham and London: Duke University Press.

Aparicio, Frances. 2019. *Negotiating Latinidad: Intralatina/O Lives in Chicago*. Urbana, Chicago and Springfield: University of Illinois Press.

Aparicio, Frances. 1998. "La vida es un Spanglish disparatero: Bilingualism in Nuyorican Poetry", En: Genevieve Fabre, ed. *European Perspectives on Hispanic Literature in the U.S*. Houston: Arte Público, 147–160.

Aparicio, Frances. 1994. "On Sub-versive Signifiers: U. S. Latina/o Writers Tropicalize English", *American Literature* 66(4): 795–801.

Aparicio, Frances, and Susana Chávez-Silverman, eds. 1997. *Tropicalizations. Transcultural Representations of Latinidad*. Hanover and London: University Press of New England.

Appadurai, Arjun. 1996. *Modernity at Large: Cultural Dimensions of Modernization*. Minneapolis: University of Minnesota Press.

Apter, Emily. 2013. *Against World Literature: On the Politics of Untranslatability*. London and New York: Verso.

Apter, Emily. 2006. *The Translation Zone: A New Comparative Literature*. Princeton and Oxford: Princeton University Press.

Arteaga, Alfred, ed. 1994. *An Other Tongue: Nation and Ethnicity in the Linguistic Borderlands*. Durham and London: Duke University Press.

Arteaga, Alfred. 1997. *Chicano Poetics: Heterotexts and Hybridities*. Cambridge, New York and Melbourne: Cambridge University Press.

Augenbraum, Harold, and Ilan Stavans, eds. 2006. *Lengua Fresca. Latinos Writing on the Edge*. Boston and New York: Mariner.

Bachmann-Medick, Doris. 2016. *Cultural Turns: New Orientations in the Study of Culture*. Berlin and Boston: De Gruyter.

Barthes, Roland. 1985/1990. "Semiología y urbanismo", En: *La aventura semiológica*. Barcelona: Paidós. Trans. Ramón Alcalde.

Barthes, Roland. 1973/1975. *The Pleasure of the Text*. New York: Hill and Wang. Trans. Richard Miller.

Bassnett, Susan. 2014. *Translation*. London and New York: Routledge.

Bassnett, Susan, and Peter Bush, eds. 2006. *The Translator as Writer*. London and New York: Continuum.

Bauman, Zygmunt. 2017. "Symptoms in Search of an Object and a Name", En: Heinrich Geiselberger, ed. *The Great Regression*. Cambridge: Polity.

Bauman, Zygmunt. 1999. *Culture as Praxis*. London: Open University/Sage.

Benedetti, Mario. 2007. *Vivir adrede*. Madrid: Alfaguara.

Benhabib, Seyla. 2018. *Exile, Statelessness and Migration*. Princeton: Princeton University Press.

Benhabib, Seyla. 2004/2005. *Los derechos de los otros. Extranjeros, residentes y ciudadanos*. Barcelona: Gedisa. Trans. Gabriel Zadunaisky.

Benjamin, Walter. 1955/1979. *One-Way Street and Other Writings*. Thetford, Norfolk: Lowe & Brydone Printers Limited. Trans. Edmund Jephcott and Kingsley Shorter.

Benjamin, Walter. 1950/2006. *Berlin Childhood around 1900*. Cambridge and London: The Belknap Press of Harvard University Press. Trans. Howard Eiland.

Berger, John. 1972. *Ways of Seeing*. London: Penguin.

Bertacco, Simona, and Nicoletta Vallorani. 2021. *The Relocation of Culture. Translation, Migration, Borders*. New York: Bloomsbury.

Bhabha, Homi K. 1996. "Culture's in-Between", In: Stuart Hall and Paul Du Gay, eds. *Questions of Cultural Identity*. London: Sage, 53–60.

Bhabha, Homi K. 1994. *The Location of Culture*. London and New York: Routledge.

Blommaert, Jan, Jan Bloomaert, Sirpa Leppänen, Päivi Pahta, and Tiina Räissänen, eds. 2012. *Dangerous Multilingualism. Northern Perspectives on Order, Purity and Normality*. London and New York: Palgrave Macmillan.

Borges, Jorge Luis. 1980/1989. "La pesadilla", En: *Siete noches, Obras completas*. Barcelona: Emecé, 221–231.

Borges, Jorge Luis. 1980/1984. "The Thousand and One Nights", *The Georgian Review* 3(Fall): 564–574. Trans. Eliot Weinberger.

Borges, Jorge Luis. 1960/1964. "Borges and I", In: *Labyrinths*. New York: New Directions. Trans. James E. Irby.

Borges, Jorge Luis. 1954/1989. "Magias parciales del *Quijote*", In: *Otras inquisiciones, Obras completas*. Barcelona: Emecé, 45–47.

Borges, Jorge Luis. 1956/1986. *Ficciones*. Madrid: Alianza.

Braschi, Giannina. 1998. *Yo-Yo Boing!* Pittsburgh: Latin American Literary Review Press.

Bromley, Roger. 2021. *Narratives of Forced Mobility and Displacement in Contemporary Literature and Culture*. New York: Palgrave Macmillan.

Brownlie, Siobhan, and Rédouane Abouddahab, eds. 2022. *Figures of the Migrant. The Role of Literature and the Arts in Representing Migration*. New York and London: Routledge.

Canagarajah, Suresh, ed. 2017. *The Routledge Handbook of Migration and Language*. London and New York: Routledge.

Canagarajah, Suresh, and Sender Dovchin. 2019. "The Everyday Politics of Translingualism as a Resistance Practice", *International Journal of Multilingualism* 16(2): 127–144.

Capildeo, Vahni. 2016. *Measures of Expatriation*. Manchester: Carcanet.

Chambers, Iain. 1994. *Migrancy, Culture, Identity*. London and New York: Routledge.

Chávez-Silverman, Susana. 2004. *Killer Crónicas: Bilingual Memories (Writing in Latinidad)*. Madison: The University of Wisconsin Press.

Ch'ien, Evelyn Nien-Ming. 2004. *Weird English*. Cambridge: Harvard University Press.

Chow, Rey. 2014. *Not Like a Native Speaker: On Languaging as a Postcolonial Experience*. New York: Columbia University Press.

Coldiron, A. E. B. 2016. "Introduction: Beyond Babel, or, the Agency of Translators in Early Modern Literature and History", *Philological Quarterly* 95(3/4): 311–323.

Cortázar, Julio, and Carol Dunlop. 1986. *Los autonautas de la cosmopista o Un viaje atemporal París-Marsella*. Barcelona: Muchnik Editores.

Coste, Didier, Christina Kkona, and Nicoletta Pireddu, eds. 2022. *Migrating Minds. Theories and Practices of Cultural Cosmopolitanism*. New York and London: Routledge.

Courtivron, Isabelle, ed. 2003. *Lives in Translation: Bilingual Writers on Identity and Creativity*. Basingstoke: Palgrave.

Craith, Máiréad Nic. 2012. *Narratives of Place, Belonging and Language. An Intercultural Perspective*. New York: Palgrave Macmillan.

Cronin, Michael. 2012. *The Expanding World: Towards a Politics of Microspection*. Winchester and Washington: Zero Books.

Cronin, Michael. 2006. *Translation and Identity*. London and New York: Routledge.

Cronin, Michael. 2000. *Across the Lines: Travel, Language, Translation*. Cork: Cork University Press.

Cronin, Michael. 1998. "The Cracked Looking Glass of Servants", *The Translator* 4(2): 145–162.

Deleuze, Gilles, and Felix Guattari. 1980/1987. *A Thousand Plateaus: Capitalism and Schizophrenia*. Minneapolis: University of Minnesota Press. Trans. Brian Massumi.

Deleuze, Gilles, and Felix Guattari. 1975/1986. *Kafka: Toward a Minor Literature*. Minneapolis and London: University of Minnesota Press. Trans. Dana Polan.

Derrida, Jaques. 1997/2001. *On Cosmopolitanism and Forgiveness*. London: Routledge. Trans. Mark Dooley and Michael Hughes.

Derrida, Jacques. 1996/1997. *El monolingüismo del otro o la prótesis del origen*. Buenos Aires: Manantial. Trans. Horacio Pons.

Doloughan, Fiona. 2017. *English as a Literature in Translation*. New York and London: Bloomsbury.

Dorfman, Ariel. 2003. "The Wandering Bigamists of Language", In: Isabelle de Courtivron, ed. *Lives in Translation: Bilingual Writers on Identity and Creativity*. Basingstoke and New York: Palgrave Macmillan, 29–37.

Dovchin, Sender, and Jerry Won Lee. 2019. "Introduction to Special Issue: 'The Ordinariness of Translinguistics'", *International Journal of Multilingualism* 16(2): 105–111.

Elliott, Bruce S., David A. Gerber, and Suanne M. Sinke, eds. 2006. *Letters across Borders: The Epistolary Practices of International Migrants*. New York: Palgrave Macmillan.

Flores, Juan, and George Yúdice. 1990. "Living Borders/Buscando America: Languages of Latino Self-Formation", *Social Text* 24: 57–84.

François, Anne Isabelle. 2017. "The Mother Tongue as Border", In: Nicola Gardini Nicola Gardini, Adriana X. Jacobs, Ben Morgan, Mohamed-Salah Omri, and Matthew Reynolds, eds. *Minding Borders: Resilient Divisions in Literature, the Body and the Academy*. Cambridge: Legenda, 115–134.

Frank, Søren. 2008. *Migration and Literature: Günter Grass, Milan Kundera, Salman Rushdie, and Jan Kjærstad*. New York: Palgrave Mcmillan.

Fusco, Coco. 1995. *English is Broken Here.: Notes on Cultural Fusion in the Americas*. New York: The New Press.

Galasso, Regina, and Ilan Stavans. 2021. "Translation as Home: A Conversation with Ilan Stavans", *Latin American Literature Today* 17.

Galasso, Regina, and Evelyn Scaramella, eds. 2019. *Avenues of Translation: The City in Iberian and Latin American Writing*. Lewisburg: Bucknell University Press.

García Canclini, Néstor. 1995. *Hybrid Cultures: Strategies for Entering and Leaving Modernity*. Minneapolis and London: University of Minnesota Press.

García, Ofelia, and Li Wei. 2014. *Translanguaging: Language, Bilingualism and Education*. London: Palgrave.

Gentzler, Edwin. 2008. *Translation and Identity in the Americas: New Directions in Translation Theory*. New York: Routledge.

Gilmour, Rachel. 2020. *Bad English: Literature, Multilingualism, and the Politics of Language in Contemporary Britain*. Manchester: Manchester University Press.

Gómez-Peña, Guillermo. 2000. *Dangerous Border Crossers: The Artist Talks Back*. London and New York: Routledge.

Gómez-Peña, Guillermo. 1996. *The New World Border*. San Francisco: City Lights.

Gramling, David. 2016. *The Invention of Monolingualism*. New York and London: Bloomsbury.

Grijelmo, Alex. 2000. *La seducción de las palabras*. Madrid: Taurus.

Hall, Stuart. 1997/2003. *Representation: Cultural Representations and Signifying Practices*. London: Sage/The Open University.

Hall, Stuart. 1996/2005. "Introduction: Who Needs Identity?" In: Stuart Hall and Paul Du Gay, eds. *Questions of Cultural Identity*. London: Sage, 1–17.

Hall, Stuart. 1993. "Cultural Identity and Diaspora", In: Patrick Williams and Laura Chrisman, eds. *Colonial Discourse & Postcolonial Theory: A Reader*. London: Harvester Wheatsheaf.

Hall, Stuart, and Paul Du Gay, eds. 1996/2005. *Questions of Cultural Identity*. London: Sage.

Heide, Markus. 2010. "Ilan Stavans's *on Borrowed Words*, Jewish-Latino/a Writing and Transnational Autobiography", *Atlantis: Journal of the Spanish Association of Anglo-American Studies* 32(1 June): 87–102.

Hoffman, Eva. 1999. "The New Nomads", In: André Aciman, ed. *Letters of Transit: Reflections on Exile, Identity, Language, and Loss*. New York: The New York Press, 39–63.

Hoffman, Eva. 1989. *Lost in Translation: A Life in a New Language*. London: Vintage.

Inghilleri, Moira. 2017. *Translation and Migration*. London and New York: Routledge.

Jaworski, Adam, and Li Wei. 2020. "Introducing *Writing (In) the City*", special issue in *Social Semiotics*. https://doi.org/10.1080/10350330.2020.1827934.

Karpinski, Eva C. 2012. *Borrowed Tongues: Life, Writing, Migration, and Translation*. Waterloo: Wilfrid Laurier University Press.

Kellman, Steven G., and Natasha Lvovich, ed. 2022. *The Routledge Handbook of Literary Translingualism*. New York and London: Routledge.

Kellman, Steven G. 2020a. *Nimble Tongues: Studies in Literary Translingualism*. West Lafayette, Indiana: Purdue University Press.

Kellman, Steven G. 2020b. "American Literature in Languages Other than English", In: Susan Belasco, ed. *A Companion to American Literature*, vol. III. Oxford: Wiley Blackwell, 349–364.

Kellman, Steven G. 2019. *The Restless Ilan Stavans. Outsider on the Inside*. Pittsburgh: University of Pittsburgh Press.

Kellman, Steven G. 2018. "Writer Speaks with Forked Tongue. Interlingual Predicaments", In: Rachel Gilmour and Tamar Steinitz, eds. *Multilingual Currents in Literature, Translation and Culture*. New York and London: Routledge, 16–33.

Kellman, Steven G. 2013. "Translating Rulfo: A Conversation with Ilan Stavans", *Translation Review* 86(1): 1–11.

Kellman, Steven G. 2003. *Switching Languages: Translingual Writers Reflect on Their Craft*. Lincoln: University of Nebraska Press.

Kellman, Steven G. 2000. *The Translingual Imagination*. Lincoln and London: University of Nebraska Press.

Kevane, Bridget, ed. 2019. *Stavans Unbound. The Critic Between Two Canons*. Boston: Academic Studies Press.

Khatibi, Abdelkebir. 1983/1990. *Love in Two Languages*. Minneapolis: University of Minnesota Press. Trans. Richard Howard.

Kohl, Katrin, and Wen-chin Ouyang. 2020. "Introducing Creative Multilingualism", In: Katrin Kohl, Katrin Kohl, Rajinder Dudrah, Andrew Gosler, Suzanne Graham, Martin Maiden, and Wen-chin Ouyang, eds. *Creative Multilingualism*. Cambridge: Open Book Publishers.

Lauret, María. 2016. *Wanderwords: Language Migration in American Literature*. New York: Bloomsbury.

Lee, Tong King, ed. 2021. *The Routledge Handbook of Translation and the City*. London and New York: Routledge.

Lee, Tong King, and Li Wei. 2021. "Translanguaging and Multilingual Creativity with English in the Sinophone World", In: Andy Kirkpatrick, ed. *Routledge*

Handbook of World Englishes, 2nd ed. New York and London: Routledge, 558–575.

Lee, Tong King, and Li Wei. 2020. "Translanguaging and Momentarity in Social Interaction", In: Anna de Fina and Alexandra Georgakopolou, eds. *The Cambridge Handbook of Discourse Studies*. Cambridge: Cambridge University Press, 394–416.

Lesser, Wendy, ed. 2004. *The Genius of Language: Fifteen Writers Reflect on Their Mother Tongues*. New York: Anchor Books.

Li, Wei. 2018. "Translanguaging as a Practical Theory of Language", *Applied Linguistics* 39(1): 9–30.

Makoni, Sinfree, and Alastair Pennycook, eds. 2007. *Disinventing and Reconstituting Languages*. Clevedon: Multilingual Matters.

Marín Hernández, David. 2022. "La traducción interdialectal como práctica domesticadora: de *Metegol* a *Futbolín*", *Onomázein* 58. https://doi.org/10.7764/onomazein.58.05.

Marín Hernández, David. 2019. "Un caso de traducción identitaria: *Le Petit Prince* en andaluz", *Meta* 64(1): 78–102.

Mbembe, Achille. 2016/2019. *Necropolitics*. Durham and London: Duke University Press. Trans. Steven Corcoran.

Mignolo, Walter D. 2000. *Local Histories/Global Designs: Coloniality, Subaltern Knowledges and Border Thinking*. Princeton: Princeton University Press.

Minh-ha, Trinh T. 2011. *Elsewhere, within Here: Immigration, Refugeeism and the Boundary Event*. New York and London: Routledge.

Montes Alcalá, Cecilia. 2019. "Bilingualism and Biculturalism. Spanish, English Spanglish?" In: Francisco A. Lomelí, Denise A. Segura, and Elyette Benjamin-Labarthe, eds. *Routledge Handbook of Chicana/o Studies*. New York and London: Routledge, 318–331.

Montes Alcalá, Cecilia. 2012. "Code-Switching in US-Latino Novels", In: Mark Sebba, Shahrzad Mahootian, and Carla Jonsson, eds. *Language Mixing and Code-Switching in Writing: Approaches to Mixed-Language Written Discourse*. London and New York: Routledge, 68–88.

Moslund, Sten Pultz. 2010. *Migration Literature and Hybridity: The Different Speeds of Transcultural Change*. New York: Palgrave.

Nail, Thomas. 2015. *The Figure of the Migrant*. Stanford: Stanford University Press.

Nergaard, Siri. 2021. *Translation and Transmigration*. London and New York: Routledge.

Newns, Lucinda. 2020. *Domestic Intersections in Contemporary Migration Fiction. Homing the Metropole*. New York: Routledge.

Nguyen, Viet Thanh, ed. 2018. *The Displaced: Refugee Writers on Refugee Lives*. New York: Abrams Press.

Onguena, Yolanda. 2014. *Pensar la mezcla*. Barcelona: Gedisa.

Otsuji, Emi, and Alastair Pennycook. 2021. "Interartefactual Translation: Metrolingualism and Resemiotization", In: Tong King Lee, ed. *The Routledge Handbook of Translation and the City*. London and New York: Routledge, 59–76.

Pennycook, Alastair. 2017. *The Cultural Politics of English as an International Language*. London and New York: Routledge.

Pennycook, Alastair. 2010. *Language as a Local Practice*. London: Routledge.

Pennycook, Alastair. 2008. "English as a Language Always in Translation", *European Journal of English Studies* 12(1): 33–47.

Pennycook, Alastair. 2007. *Global Englishes and Transcultural Flows*. Abingdon and New York: Routledge.

Pennycook, Alastair, and Emi Otsuji. 2015. *Metrolingualism: Language and the City*. London: Routledge.

Polezzi, Loredana. 2012. "Translation and Migration", *Translation Studies* 5(3): 345–368.

Polezzi, Loredana. 2006. "Translation, Travel, Migration", *The Translator* 12(2): 169–188.

Porras Blanco, Juan. 2017. *Er Prinzipito*. Necarsteinach: Tintenfass.

Pratt, Mary Louise. 2016. "Lessons for Losing", *The New Centennial Review: Translation and the Global Humanities* 16(1): 245–251.

Pratt, Mary Louise. 2013. "Travelling Languages: Toward a Geolinguistic Imagination", *Muiraquitã*, PPGLI-UFAC 2(1 July/December): 244–262.

Pratt, Mary Louise. 2012. "'If English was Good Enough for Jesus': Monolingüismo y mala fe", *Critical Multilingualism Studies* 1(1): 12–30.

Pratt, Mary Louise. 2011. "Comparative Literature and the Global Languagescape", In: Ali Behdad and Dominic Thomas, eds. *A Companion to Comparative Literature*. Oxford: Wiley-Blackwell, 273–295.

Pratt, Mary Louise. 2010. "Response", Translation Studies Forum: Cultural Translation. *Translation Studies* 3(1): 94–110.

Pratt, Mary Louise. 2003. "Building a New Public Idea about Language", *Profession*. MLA: 110–119.

Pratt, Mary Louise. 2002. "The Traffic in Meaning: Translation, Contagion, Infiltration", *Profession*. MLA: 25–36.

Pratt, Mary Louise. 1992. *Imperial Eyes: Travel Writing and Transculturation*. London and New York: Routledge.

Pratt, Mary Louise. 1987. "Linguistic Utopias", In: Nigel Fabb, Derek Attridge, Alan Durant, and Colin MacCabe, eds. *The Linguistics of Writing*. Manchester: Manchester University Press, 48–66.

Rabourdin, Caroline. 2020. *Sense in Translation: Essays on the Bilingual Body*. London and New York: Routledge.

Rabourdin, Caroline. 2016. "Walking and Writing: Paul Auster's Map of the Tower of Babel", In: Emmanuelle Peraldo, ed. *Literature and Geography: The Writing of Space through History*. Cambridge: Cambridge Scholars Publishing, 222–233.

Rudin, Ernst. 1996. *Tender Accents of Sound. Spanish in the Chicano Novel in English*. Tempe: Bilingual Press/Editorial Bilingüe.

Rose, Kate, ed. 2020. *Displaced: Literature of Indigeneity, Migration and Trauma*. New York and London: Routledge.

Rushdie, Salman. 2003. *Step Across this Line: Collected Nonfiction 1992–2002*. New York: Modern Library.

Rushdie, Salman. 2000. "In Defence of the Novel, Yet Again", In: *Step Across This Line: Collected Non-Fiction 1992–2002*. London: Vintage, 2003, 54–63.

Rushdie, Salman. 1992. *Imaginary Homelands: Essays and Criticism, 1981–1991*. London: Penguin/Granta.

Sánchez Marta, E. 2019. *A Translational Turn: Latinx Literature into the Mainstream*. Pittsburg: University of Pittsburg Press.

Said, Edward. 2001. *Reflexions on Exile and Other Essays*. Cambridge: Harvard University Press.

Said, Edward. 1999. *Out of Place: A Memoir*. London: Granta.

Said, Edward. 1993. *Culture and Imperialism*. London and New York: Vintage.

Seyhan, Azade. 2014. "The Translated City: Immigrants, Minorities, Diasporans, and Cosmopolitans", In: Kevin McNamara, ed. *The Cambridge Companion to the City in Literature*. New York: Cambridge University Press, 216–232.

Seyhan, Azade. 2001. *Writing Outside the Nation*. Princeton: Princeton University Press.

Shea, Renee H., and Edwidge Danticat. 1996. "The Dangerous Job of Edwidge Danticat: An Interview", *Callaloo* 19(2): 382–389.

Simon, Sherry. 2019. *Translation Sites: A Field Guide*. London and New York: Routledge.

Simon, Sherry. 2012. *Cities in Translation: Intersections of Language and Memory*. London and New York: Routledge.

Sommer, Doris. 2004. *Bilingual Aesthetics: A New Sentimental Education*. Durham: Duke University Press.

Sommer, Doris, ed. 2003. *Bilingual Games: Some Literary Investigations*. New York: Palgrave.

Spivak, Gayatri Chakravorty. 1999. *A Critique of Postcolonial Reason: Towards a History of the Vanishing Present*. New York: Routledge.

Spivak, Gayatri Chakravorty. 1993. "The Politics of Translation", In: *Outside in the Teaching Machine*. London: Routledge.

Spoturno, María Laura. 2021. "On *Borderlands* and Translation. The Spanish Versions of Gloria Anzaldúa's Seminal Work", En: Luise von Flotow y Hala Kamal, eds. *The Routledge Handbook of Translation, Feminism and Gender*. London and New York: Routledge, 239–251.

Spoturno, María Laura. 2019. "La conquista del espacio enunciativo. Un estudio de las notas en la traducción al español de *Borderlands/La Frontera*", *Lengua y habla* 23(enero–diciembre): 360–379.

Stavans, Ilan. 2021a. *Selected Translations 2000–2020*. Pittsburgh: University of Pittsburgh Press.

Stavans, Ilan. 2021b. *What is American Literature?* New York: Oxford University Press.

Stavans, Ilan. 2021c. *Jewish Literature: A Very Short Introduction*. New York: Oxford University Press.

Stavans, Ilan. 2021d. *Alicia's Adventuras in Wonderlandia*. Dundee: Evertype.

Stavans, Ilan. 2021e. "'Clean, fix, and Grant Splendor': The Making of *Diccionario de Autoridades*", *International Journal of Lexicography*, 1–11; ecab025. https://doi.org/10.1093/ijl/ecab025.

Stavans, Ilan. 2020a. "Self-Translation como survival mecanismo", *Ínsula* 885 septiembre, número especial editado por Ángel Esteban: 13–15.

Stavans, Ilan. 2020b. *How Yiddish Changed America How America Changed Yiddish*. New York: Restless Books.

Stavans, Ilan, ed. 2020c. *The Oxford Handbook of Latino Studies*. New York: Oxford University Press.

Stavans, Ilan. 2020d. "Foreward", In: Frederick Luis Aldama and Tess O'Dwyer, eds. *Poets, Philosophers, Lovers: On the Writings of Giannina Braschi*. Pittsburgh: University of Pittsburgh Press, xi–xii.

Stavans, Ilan. 2020e. *Popol Vuh*. New York: Restless Books.

Stavans, Ilan. 2018a. *On Self-Translation: Meditations on Language*. Albany: State University of New York Press.

Stavans, Ilan. 2018b. *The Wall*. Pittsburgh: University of Pittsburg Press.

Stavans, Ilan. 2018c. *Sor Juana: Or, the Persistence of Pop*. Tucson: The University of Arizona Press.

Stavans, Ilan. 2017. *I Love My Selfie*. Durham and London: Duke University Press.

Stavans, Ilan. 2016. *El Little Príncipe*. Necarsteinach: Tintenfass.

Stavans, Ilan. 2014. *A Most Imperfect Union: A Contrarian History of the United States*. New York: Basic Books.

Stavans, Ilan. 2013. *The United States of Mestizo*. Montgomery: New South Books.

Stavans, Ilan. 2012. "On Being Misunderstood", *Translation Review* 84(1): 10–15.

Stavans, Ilan. 2008a. *Knowledge and Censorship: Con Verónica Albín*. New York: Palgrave Macmillan.

Stavans, Ilan, ed. 2008b. *Spanglish*. Westport: Greenwood Press.

Stavans, Ilan. 2003. *Spanglish: The Making of a New American Language*. New York: HarperCollins.

Stavans, Ilan. 2002. *On Borrowed Words: A Memoir of Language*. New York: Penguin.

Stavans, Ilan. 2001. *The Inveterate Dreamer: Essays and Conversations on Jewish Culture*. Lincoln and London: University of Nebraska Press.

Stavans, Ilan, ed. 1999. *Mutual Impressions: Writers from the Americas Reading One Another*. Durham and London: Duke University Press.

Stavans, Ilan. 1996. *Art and Anger: Essays on Politics and the Imagination*. New York: Palgrave.

Stavans, Ilan, and Juan Villoro. 2014. *El ojo en la nuca*. Barcelona: Anagrama.

Stavans, Ilan, and Marc Charron. 2004. "*Don Quijote* in Spanglish. Translation and Appropriation", *TTR: Traduction, Terminologie, Redaction* 17(1): 183–194.

Stavans, Ilan, and Marcelo Brodsky. 2016. *Once @ 9:53 am: Terror en Buenos Aires*. University Park: Pennsylvania State University Press.

Stavans, Ilan, and Steve Sheinkin. 2012. *El Iluminado*. New York: Basic Books.

Tang, Jenna. 2021. "Reimagining the Classics: A Conversation with Publisher Ilan Stavans", World Literature Today. https://www.worldliteraturetoday.org/blog/interviews/reimagining-classics-conversation-publisher-ilan-stavans-jenna-tang.

Tilbe, Ali, M. Rania, and Rafik Khalil, eds. 2019. *Culture, Literature and Migration*. London: Transnational Press.

Todorov, Tzvetan. 2007. "What is Literature For?", *New Literary History* 38(1): 13–32.

Tong, Haoran. 2021. "The Poet's Languages: A Conversation between Ilan Stavans and Haoran Tong", *The Common* Online, 17 August. https://www.thecommononline.org/the-poets-languages-a-conversation-between-ilan-stavans-and-haoran-tong/.

Urry, John. 2004. *Global Complexity*. Cambridge: Polity Press.

Vallejo, Irene. 2019/2021. *El infinito en un junco. La invención de los libros en el mundo antiguo.* Madrid: Siruela.

Vidal Claramonte, Mª Carmen África. 2021. *Traducción y literatura translingüe. Voces latinas en Estados Unidos.* Madrid and Frankfurt: Vervuert Iberoamericana.

Vidal Claramonte, Mª Carmen África, and Ilan Stavans. 2022. "On Memes as Semiotic Hand-Grenades: A Conversation", In: Tong King Lee and Dingkun Wang, eds. *Translation and Social Media Communication in the Age of the Pandemic*. London and New York: Routledge, 98–114.

Waisman, Sergio. 2005. *Borges y la traducción.* Córdoba: Adriana Hidalgo editora. Trans. Marcelo Cohen.

Walkowitz, Rebecca L. 2015. *Born Translated: The Contemporary Novel in an Age of World Literature.* New York: Columbia University Press.

Walkowitz, Rebecca L. 2006a. *Cosmopolitan Styles: Modernism Beyond the Nation.* New York: Columbia University Press.

Walkowitz, Rebecca L., ed. 2006b. *Immigrant Fictions: Contemporary Literature in an Age of Globalization, Contemporary Literature*, Winter, 27, 4. The University of Wisconsin Press.

Wilson, Rita. 2021. "Changing Places: Translation Narratives of Migration, Cultural Memory, and Belonging", In: Susannah Radstone and Rita Wilson, eds. *Translating Worlds. Migration, Memory, and Culture.* London and New York: Routledge, 148–163.

Wilson, Rita. 2018. "Narrating the Polyphonic City: Translation and Identity in Translingual/Transcultural Writing", In: Rachael Gilmour and Tamar Steinitz, eds. *Multilingual Currents in Literature, Translation, and Culture.* New York and London: Routledge, 55–80.

Wilson, Rita. 2011. "Cultural Mediation through Translingual Narrative", *Target* 23(2): 235–250.

Woodsworth, Judith, ed. 2022. *Translation and the Global City: Bridges and Gateways.* New York and London: Routledge.

Yildiz, Yasemin. 2012. *Beyond the Mother Tongue: The Postmonolingual Condition.* New York: Fordham University Press.

Index

Printed in the United States
by Baker & Taylor Publisher Services

Printed in the United States
by Baker & Taylor Publisher Services